ANCILLARY RELIEF PILOT SCHEME – A PRACTICE GUIDE

ANCILLARY RELIEF PILOT SCHEME – A PRACTICE GUIDE

David Burrows
Solicitor-Advocate (Higher Courts Civil)

 **Family Law**

1997

Published by Family Law
an imprint of Jordan Publishing Limited
21 St Thomas Street
Bristol BS1 6JS

© Jordan Publishing Limited 1997

British Library Cataloguing-in-Publication Data
A catalogue record for this book is available from the British Library.

ISBN 0 85308 446 7

Typeset by Mendip Communications Ltd, Frome, Somerset
Printed in Great Britain by Hobbs the Printers Ltd of Southampton

PREFACE

In his Foreword to the Practitioner's Guide to the Scheme,[1] Thorpe LJ considered that it was for practitioners to ensure that the Scheme 'does not founder as a result of ignorance or reactionary rejection'. It is to be hoped that what follows goes some way to fend off ignorance. In principle the Scheme is most welcome: any procedural development which encourages settlement and saves costs, whilst still preserving fairness, deserves praise. However, it is difficult not to be disappointed by a number of aspects of the Scheme: the quality of some of the drafting of the rules; the apparent disregard for certain fundamental rules of evidence, such as discovery and legal professional privilege; and difficulties in applying the Scheme to claims beyond those for the mainstream periodical payments, lump sum and property adjustment orders. Rule drafting which lacks attention to detail only increases expense to the client – as lawyers argue out points of procedural detail – rather than saving costs.

The more fundamental question which family lawyers face in the wake of the Woolf Report[2] is the issue of whether or not it is intended that procedures in the family courts are to become more inquisitorial. The Scheme is an important development in the debate on this subject. Perhaps two pleas may be permitted at this stage. First, that judges and district judges in their concern to be interventionist recall the fact that, like all of us, their object – especially in a family jurisdiction – is to serve the litigant by seeking equity between the parties: needless expense to the client can be caused, for example, by over-insistence on rigid time-tables, front-loading of proceedings and judicial insistence on court attendances which are not completely necessary. Secondly, judges could be the apex of a co-operative venture which aims to achieve a fair result for the parties. As such, advocate and judge alike can seek to maintain a mutual respect. The possibility of our judges and advocates developing the mutually dismissive relationship which can occur in the French court system, for example, must surely be avoided.

Common-law rules of evidence have been developed over centuries to assist in achieving justice and for the protection of the parties. Parts of the new rules and *Practice Direction: Ancillary Relief Procedure: Pilot Scheme (16 June 1997)* [1997] 2 FLR 304 are evidence of attempts by practice direction or rule – that is with minimal or no debate – to alter important protection for parties to court proceedings derived from time-honoured common-law remedies. Without debate or primary legislation that should surely not be possible.

My sincere thanks to Jordans for agreeing at such short notice to a proposal

---

1 *Ancillary Relief Pilot Scheme: Practitioners' Guide* (SFLA and FLBA, August 1996; and see **1.1** below).
2 *Access to Justice: Final Report* by Lord Woolf MR (HMSO, July 1996).

for this book and for their efforts to publish it as quickly as they could. I am grateful to Lucienne and Raymond Monget-Sarrail for their kindness during my week in Le Muy in the South of France whilst I wrote the text. And, most of all, acknowledgement is due to the members of the Advisory Group – volunteers all – who developed the ideas which underlie the Scheme.

The law is stated as I understand it to be at August 1997.

DAVID BURROWS
Bristol, August 1997

CONTENTS

TABLE OF CASES

References are to paragraph numbers

TABLE OF STATUTES

References are to paragraph numbers

TABLE OF STATUTORY INSTRUMENTS

References are to paragraph numbers; *italic* references are to page numbers

LIST OF COURTS TO WHICH THE ANCILLARY RELIEF PILOT SCHEME APPLIES

(1)   The Principal Registry of the Family Division
(2)   The divorce county courts listed below
(3)   The High Court in a district registry mentioned below

The courts

Barnsley	Northampton
Bath	Salford
Blackwood	Southampton
Bolton	Southport
Boston	Stafford
Bow	Staines
Bristol	Stoke-on-Trent
Bury	Taunton
Crewe	Teesside
Guildford	Trowbridge
Harrogate	Tunbridge Wells
Hertford	Willesden
Kingston	Wrexham
Maidstone	

Chapter 1

INTRODUCTION

BACKGROUND TO THE SCHEME

1.1 The Ancillary Relief Pilot Scheme started life as a voluntary initiative developed by a committee chaired by Thorpe LJ (which later became the Lord Chancellor's Ancillary Relief Advisory Group). That committee eventually put forward recommendations which were then incorporated into a 'Draft Rule' annexed to a President's Direction dated 25 July 1996[1], published as a judicial guide. A practitioner's guide ('the Guide')[2] included the Draft Rule and Direction, and was accompanied by a Commentary on Pilot Scheme Procedure ('the Commentary'), prepared by members of the Group representing the Solicitors Family Law Association and the Family Law Bar Association. The Scheme was limited to a specific number of courts[3] and applied to all ancillary relief applications issued in those courts on and after 1 October 1996. With effect from 21 April 1997, it has been incorporated formally into the Family Proceedings Rules 1991[4] by the Family Proceedings (Amendment) (No 2) Rules 1997[5]; but only after the Lord Chancellor had given himself powers to set up pilot schemes in the Civil Procedure Act 1997[6].

1.2 In his Foreword to the Guide, Thorpe LJ praised the 'flexibility of the judicial powers' available under the Matrimonial Causes Act 1973, ss 22–25C. He criticised 'the practices and procedures by which some cases are prepared for trial' and then continued:

> 'The underlying basis of trust was that litigants and their lawyers could be relied upon to prepare their cases sensibly and with due regard to proportionality . . . It is abundantly obvious in this field, as in the wider field of civil litigation[7], that there must be far stricter court control together with court led mediation and a proper emphasis on the escalating costs bills. The new procedures have been designed to meet these objectives.'

---

1 The text of the President's Direction can be found at Appendix 2 and is published at [1996] 2 FLR 368.

2 *Ancillary Relief Pilot Scheme: Practitioner's Guide* by Lord Chancellor's Advisory Group on Ancillary Relief (August 1996, published by SFLA and FLBA).

3 For a list of the courts, see the Family Proceedings (Amendment) (No 2) Rules 1997, SI 1997/1056, para 4/2.71(2).

4 Family Proceedings Rules 1991, rr 2.71–2.77.

5 SI 1997/1056, para 4.

6 Schedule 2, para 3 which effectively gives the Lord Chancellor powers to introduce pilot schemes: 'different provision for different cases or different areas, including different provision—(a) for a specific court, or (b) for specific proceedings, or a specific jurisdiction'.

7 Cf **1.5** et seq below.

'Objectives' of the Scheme

1.3   The President's Direction defined the 'objective' of the Scheme, as then drafted, as follows:

> 'To reduce delay, facilitate settlements, limit costs incurred by the parties to the proceedings and provide the court with much greater control over the conduct of proceedings than exists at present.'

1.4   In what follows, the Scheme will first be considered in outline. What remains of pre-existing practice and procedure will be assessed in the context of the Scheme. Next, procedure under the Scheme will be considered in detail and by contrast with the existing procedures. The subject of costs, such a central concern of the Scheme, will be looked at in the light of the new and the old procedures. Before this, it may be helpful to look at the background to the Scheme and the context in which it has been developed.

CONTEXT SURROUNDING THE COMMITTEE'S DISCUSSIONS

Lord Woolf's report

1.5   Thorpe LJ's committee started its deliberations against a background of increasing judicial concern at the escalating costs of litigation in all Divisions of the High Court and in county courts. In March 1994, a committee under Lord Woolf had been set up to review rules and procedure in civil courts, a primary aim of the committee being 'to improve access to justice and reduce the cost of litigation'. One of the main factors in this was the view that there needed to be more judicial control of the pace of litigation; for litigation delayed could lead to injustice, and, almost by definition, delays lead to increased costs.

1.6   Lord Woolf's committee delivered an interim report[8] in June 1995 which led to *Access to Justice: Final Report* by Lord Woolf MR (HMSO, July 1996) ('the Woolf Report'). That report proposes a new 'landscape of civil litigation . . . embodying the principles of equality, economy, proportionality and expedition which are fundamental to an effective contemporary system of justice'[9] and is accompanied by a draft set of rules. Although the Scheme proposed by the Woolf Report is specifically not intended to apply to family proceedings[10], its effects will be felt widely by family lawyers and it has plainly

---

8 *Access to Justice: Interim Report* by Lord Woolf MR (HMSO, June 1995).

9 Section 1, para 8.

10 The present civil proceedings rules (Rules of the Supreme Court 1965 and County Court Rules 1981) apply to the family proceedings covered by the Family Proceedings Rules 1991, save where they are inconsistent with those rules: Family Proceedings Rules 1991, r 1.3(1).

influenced Thorpe LJ and the Lord Chancellor's Ancillary Relief Advisory Group. If the recommendations of the Woolf Report are introduced,[11] it is inconceivable that reforms along similar lines will not be introduced in the family courts; and the Pilot Scheme is evidence of a move towards such reforms.

Case management

1.7 While Lord Woolf's enquiries were already under way, all Divisions of the High Court published Practice Directions on case management. In the Family Division, *Practice Direction of 31 January 1995 (Case Management)* [1995] 1 FLR 456, [1995] 1 WLR 332, although unexceptional in its aims, has proved disappointing in practice; and no attempt has been made to ensure its operation with anything like uniformity.

Court control

1.8 In ancillary relief proceedings, through the Matrimonial Causes Act 1973, s 25(1)[12], Parliament has imposed upon the courts a duty to enquire into the financial circumstances of a divorce, before making any order for financial relief. However, the rules give no clear guidance for the parties or the judiciary in support of this inquisitorial function[13]; although evidence is beginning to emerge that the High Court judiciary are starting to envisage for the court a more inquisitorial mode. The words of Thorpe J[14], himself, in *F v F (Ancillary Relief: Substantial Assets)*[15] summarise this process[16]:

> 'I think that it is timely to stress that ancillary relief applications in this Division are not purely adversarial proceedings. The court has an independent duty to discharge the function imposed by statute. The court has from that duty the power to investigate and the power to ensure compliance with the duty of full and frank disclosure owed by the litigants.'[17]

---

11 The previous government gave itself powers in the Civil Procedure Act 1997 consistent with the Woolf Report.

12 'It shall be the duty of the court in deciding whether to exercise its powers . . . to have regard to all the circumstances of the case . . .'; and see the assessment of the meaning of these words in the context of disclosure as between the parties by Lord Brandon in *Jenkins v Livesey (formerly Jenkins)* [1985] AC 424, sub nom *Livesey (formerly Jenkins) v Jenkins* [1985] FLR 813, HL.

13 Save in the little used Family Proceedings Rules 1991, r 2.62(4).

14 As he then was.

15 [1995] 2 FLR 45. The dictum here quoted follows immediately upon a brief description by Thorpe J of the meetings of what was shortly to become the Lord Chancellor's Advisory Group on Ancillary Relief under the judge's chairmanship.

16 And see eg the approach of Wilson J to joinder of trustees in a case involving substantial funds transferred by a husband to a discretionary trust whose objects excluded the wife in *T v T and Others (Joinder of Third Parties)* [1996] 2 FLR 357: 'A crucial matter for my determination will be to evaluate the real control over the assets of this trust . . . A duty has been imposed upon the court in these proceedings. I have to get to the bottom of the reality behind this trust' (per Wilson J at 365F and 366E).

17 [1995] 2 FLR 45 at 70A.

And for the future? The closing words of Thorpe J encapsulate his own committee's and Lord Woolf's approach:

> 'Everybody, as it seems to me, has fought this good fight according to the practices which hitherto have prevailed. All I question is whether those practices should continue to prevail, and whether we do not need to change the approach and the practice so that the preparation will be undertaken more co-operatively and less contentiously and the resulting bills consequently reduced.'[18]

1.9   The potential for important change in our court processes suggested by those words is difficult to exaggerate. Well managed, these changes ought only to improve prospects for the parties and for a fair disposal of the case conducted expeditiously and cost-effectively (within the bounds demanded by the parties' respective financial and other circumstances). But it involves a fundamental shift from the adversarial to the inquisitorial mode of procedure[19].

Costs savings

1.10   Reported cases over the past year or so make it clear that the judiciary are already more than conscious of the significance of costs orders[20]. The incidence of costs in litigation generally is a major concern of the Woolf Report. Were the research to be done, it would probably establish that the diversion of funds from private individuals to lawyers as a result of the costs of litigation is a perceptible drain on this country's economy: the more so when it is recalled that the rate of family breakdown in England and Wales is so high. Anything that can be done equitably to reduce that drain must surely be to the general good.

---

18 [1995] 2 FLR 45 at 71D.

19 For further consideration of this question see **9.1** et seq.

20 A number of these cases are considered at **7.7** et seq.

Chapter 2

THE PILOT SCHEME IN OPERATION

INTRODUCTION

2.1   The Pilot Scheme is the generic term for a new set of rules superimposed upon the existing Family Proceedings Rules 1991 by the Family Proceedings (Amendment) (No 2) Rules 1997. Those rules which are unamended by the Scheme continue in operation in relation to applications under the Scheme; and so too do the many practice directions and the legal principles enunciated by judges since the coming into operation of the Matrimonial Causes Act 1973 (and its predecessor) in January 1971. Some of these judicial legal principles are likely to assume additional prominence under the Scheme[1], particularly where orders for costs are concerned.

The pre-existing procedure

2.2   The pre-existing procedure is set out in the Family Proceedings Rules 1991[2] and applies to applications for ancillary relief under the Matrimonial Causes Act 1973 commenced in all courts not covered by the Scheme. In the context of these Rules, 'ancillary relief' is described as[3]:

'(a) an avoidance of disposition order[4],
(b) a financial provision order[5],
(c) an order for maintenance pending suit[6],
(d) a property adjustment order[7], or
(e) a variation order[8].'

Process is commenced by the claim being included in a spouse's petition or answer, which claim is then triggered by the filing of Form M13[9] or by a spouse, who has not filed a petition or answer, filing an originating

---

1 See eg *Edgar v Edgar* (1981) FLR 19, [1981] 1 WLR 1410, CA (what effect to be given by the courts to agreements reached by parties outside the court process) and see **7.11** below; *Gojkovic v Gojkovic (No 2)* [1992] Fam 40, [1991] 2 FLR 233, CA (the extent to which costs should follow the event in ancillary relief proceedings): see **7.7** below.

2 Rules 2.52–2.71.

3 Family Proceedings Rules 1991, r 1.2(1).

4 Ie an order under the Matrimonial Causes Act 1973, s 37(2)(b) or (c).

5 Ibid, s 23 (ie lump sum and periodical payments).

6 Ibid, s 22.

7 Ibid, s 23. An order for sale of property does not appear in this list since, it will be recalled, such an order can only be made ancillary to orders for a lump sum, property adjustment or secured periodical payments: ibid, s 24A(1).

8 Ibid, s 31.

9 Family Proceedings Rules 1991, r 2.58(1).

application in Form M11[10]. Either originating application must be supported by an affidavit in which the applicant sets out 'full particulars of his property and income'[11], 'the facts relied on in support of the application'[12] and certain other details of his case[13]. The procedure between filing of the application and the hearing varies from court to court. In the process, parties may request further information of one another, which (if not provided) may be directed by a district judge[14]. Third parties may be required to produce documents to the court[15] or to appear[16]; and at the hearing it is the duty of the district judge to 'investigate the allegations made in support of and in answer to the application'.

Outline of procedure under the Scheme

2.3   One of the features of the Scheme, immediately discernible, is the clarity with which its draftsmen have provided for the progress of a case from application to final hearing. They have completely removed the vagueness of the existing procedures, which have themselves spawned a variety of local practices and procedures which are quite outside the Family Proceedings Rules 1991. However, it is rare – perhaps unique – in English law-making, to have parallel sets of provisions existing side-by-side in the same set of rules: more usually where rules are disapplied they are repealed or amended with universal effect so that the rules, as amended, can be read as a composite set of provisions. This will not be the case for anyone taking part in the Scheme. They will have to read the new rules with the old alongside[17]; and many important considerations of principle remain as applicable to applications under the Scheme as under existing procedures.

2.4   In outline, proceedings under the Scheme[18] are as follows:

---

10 Family Proceedings Rules 1991, r 2.53(3).
11 Ibid, r 2.58(2) and (3).
12 It is noteworthy that this form of words applies only to the applicant and that it falls well short of the requirements for full relevant disclosure set out in *Jenkins v Livesey (formerly Jenkins)* [1985] AC 424, sub nom *Livesey (formerly Jenkins) v Jenkins* [1985] FLR 813, HL. A layman applying to the court could be forgiven for not realising that he should state his marital intentions, give details of any expected improvement in his financial position or (where relevant) give information about his cohabitant or new wife: these are scarcely factors 'in support' of an application.
13 Ibid, r 2.59(1) sets out details of certain matters which must be included in the affidavit in applications for property adjustment orders, variations of settlement and avoidance of disposition.
14 Ibid, r 2.63.
15 Ibid, r 2.62(7)–(9).
16 Rules of the Supreme Court 1965, Ord 38, r 14 (subpoena in High Court); County Court Rules 1981, Ord 20, r 12 (witness summonses in the county courts).
17 Appendix 2 sets out the existing rules with new rules superimposed.
18 See also the Procedural Guide at Appendix 1.

Application in Forms A or B
Applications are commenced on a simplified form of application[19]: Form A (ancillary relief) or Form B (applications under the Matrimonial Causes Act 1973, s 10(2) which, for the purposes of this procedure, has been added to the list of proceedings for ancillary relief). Upon issue of the application, a 'First Appointment' is fixed which must be 10 to 14 weeks ahead.

Form E – sworn statement of means
Five weeks before the First Appointment both parties file, and serve on each other, Form E (statement of means and of their case)[20].

First Appointment
The objective of the first appointment[21] is to define the issues and the saving of costs. At that appointment the district judge gives directions including referral of the application for a Financial Dispute Resolution ('FDR').

Financial Dispute Resolution
The FDR appointment[22] is intended to be 'a meeting held for the purposes of conciliation' at which the district judge may try to assist the parties to reach agreement (that district judge then has no further involvement in the case, save at any further FDR).

Hearing
If no agreement is reached at the FDR the district judge can give directions for the final hearing[23]; and the parties proceed accordingly. The attention to procedural detail evident in the scheme disappears and the parties and their representatives are left at the mercy of the practice of individual courts, district judges and judges; save that before the hearing the parties must, sequentially, file details of the order they seek from the court[24].

Costs
The Scheme stresses its concern over costs by requiring that at every hearing each party shall produce a written estimate of costs[25].

---

19 Family Proceedings Rules 1991 (as amended by Family Proceedings (Amendment) (No 2) Rules 1997, SI 1997/1056), r 2.72.
20 Ibid, r 2.73.
21 Ibid, r 2.74(1).
22 Ibid, r 2.75.
23 Ibid, rr 2.74(1)(d)(iii) and 2.75(1)(d).
24 Ibid, r 2.77.
25 Ibid, r 2.76.

THE SCHEME AND THE FAMILY PROCEEDINGS RULES

The effect of the amendment rules

2.5   The procedural machinery of the Scheme operates to disapply certain rules in the Family Proceedings Rules 1991 and slightly to amend others[26]. The disapplied rules are replaced and developed by the amendment rules, whilst the remainder of the rules continue to be operative in respect of all applications, whether or not under the Scheme[27]. The following table shows the rules which are disapplied, the effect of the original rule and a note on what replaces them.

Table 1: Existing Family Proceedings Rules 1991 disapplied by the Scheme

FPR 1991 disapplied	Effect of disapplied rule	Amendment rule and its operation
2.45(2),(3)	Exchange of affidavits: application under MCA 1973, s 10(2)	Affidavits are replaced by Form E: r 2.73 and App 1A
2.58(2), (3)	Exchange of affidavits in applications for ancillary relief	
2.59(1)	Contents of affidavit of means	Rule 2.73(2) sets out exactly what information will be required by the court and this is provided for in Form E
2.62(1) and (3)	Notice of appointment and hearing before district judge	Fixing of appointments under the Scheme is on a different basis, more tightly controlled by the court
2.62(5)–(6)	Directions by district judge: in practice these depend considerably on local practice	Directions by the district judge are central to the operation of the scheme: eg r 2.74(1) and r 2.75(1)(d)
2.63	Requests for further information	Entirely under the control of the district judge: r 2.74(1)(a); and discovery is strictly limited: r 2.73(3)
2.71(1)	Information as to benefit under a pension scheme in affidavit of means	To be included in Form E: r 2.73(2)(f)(iii)

---

26 Family Proceedings Rules 1991, r 2.71(3).

27 At Appendix 2 the rules as amended are shown alongside the old rules.

In addition, r 2.58(1) (issue of application in Form M13) applies subject to the new rr 2.72 to 2.77[28]. References to service of applications under r 2.55 (issue of applications in Form M11 or M12) are deleted for the purposes of the Scheme[29]. Words are omitted from, and substituted in, r 2.60(1) (service on a person named in affidavit[30] as allegedly involved in adultery or 'an improper association' with the other spouse) to make it consistent with the Scheme[31]. Finally, for the purposes of applications under the Scheme references in the rules to Forms M11, M12, M13 or M14 are now to Forms A, B or F[32]; but, unfortunately, references to affidavits of means have not been deleted to make way for Form E.

Continuing application of Family Proceedings Rules 1991

2.6   Thus, of the earlier rules, the following continue to affect procedure under the Scheme:

(a)   Form A, like Forms M11 and M13, must include the requirements set out in the Family Proceedings Rules 1991, r 2.59(2)–(5): for example, details of land registration and mortgagees must be included in Form A and it must be served on the mortgagees[33].

(b)   Rule 2.61 statements will still be required in the case of applications which are settled and where a consent application is to be submitted to the court; although it is to be hoped that the provision which enables the court to dispense with a r 2.61 statement 'where all or any of the parties attend the hearing of an application for financial relief'[34] will be extended to the FDR especially as it is envisaged that at that appointment 'the court may make such consent order as may be appropriate'[35].

---

28 Family Proceedings Rules 1991, r 2.71(3)(c). This rule is difficult to understand, since the new rules seem completely to replace r 2.58(1).

29 Ibid, r 2.71(3)(b).

30 The word 'affidavit' has been retained when the draftsman appears to have intended a reference to Form E.

31 Family Proceedings Rules 1991, r 2.71(3)(d).

32 Ibid, r 2.71(3)(f).

33 Under Family Proceedings Rules 1991, r 2.59(4) following service of Form A the mortgagee is able to apply to the court for a copy 'of the applicant's affidavit'. This must be taken to mean Form E, although no reference to such an amendment is made in r 2.71(3).

34 Family Proceedings Rules 1991, r 2.61(3).

35 Ibid, r 2.75(1)(d).

(c)   Production appointments[36] will remain available[37]. Such appointments should, perhaps, be applied for (wherever possible) at the first appointment, or following an FDR. Such application should be made on notice[38], save in cases of emergency.

(d)   The application may be referred by the district judge to a judge[39] who then has the same powers as a district judge to give directions[40].

(e)   Finally, it should be recalled that any appropriate Rules of the Supreme Court 1965 or County Court Rules 1981 remain applicable, subject to the Family Proceedings Rules 1991, r 1.3(1)[41]: for example the provisions of Rules of the Supreme Court 1965, Ord 38, Part IV (expert evidence) remain as important as ever, and Ord 62 (with the Supreme Court Act 1981, s 51) is the sole basis for the court to deal with orders for costs; whilst Ord 40 (court appointed experts) is gaining currency[42].

The *vires* of the Scheme

2.7   Following the coming into operation of the 'draft rules' there were doubts about whether or not there was power in the President, by Practice Direction, to alter court rules approved by Parliament[43]. Any doubts, as to the *vires* of the Scheme as a whole, are put to rest by the amendment rules. As to the original Scheme, there is incorporated into the amendment rules a provision that retrospectively gives legitimacy to all that had been done, prior to 21 April 1997, under the old draft rules and the President's Direction.

---

36 Family Proceedings Rules 1991, r 2.62(7)–(9).

37 Although it should be recalled that an accelerated procedure is available by means of issue of a subpoena duces tecum (High Court) or witness summons which does not require the leave of the court in the same way as the production appointment (*Khanna v Lovell White Durrant (a firm)* [1994] 4 All ER 267, Sir Donald Nicholls V-C).

38 *B v B (Production Appointment: Procedure)* [1995] 1 FLR 913, Thorpe J.

39 Family Proceedings Rules 1991, r 2.65.

40 Ibid, r 2.66(4) and 2.74(3) (by amendment of r 2.66(4) for the purposes of the Scheme by r 2.71(3)).

41 Rule 1.3(1) applies Rules of the Supreme Court 1965 and County Court Rules 1981 to family proceedings, save where they are inconsistent with Family Proceedings Rules 1991.

42 *Re K (Contact: Psychiatric Report)* [1995] 2 FLR 432, CA (a children case); *Abbey National Mortgagees Plc v Key Surveyors Nationwide Ltd and Others* [1996] 1 WLR 1534, CA (valuation evidence); and see **4.24** et seq below.

43 And see *Langley v North West Area Health Authority* [1991] 1 WLR 697, CA.

Chapter 3

COMMENCEMENT OF PROCEEDINGS FOR ANCILLARY RELIEF

THE APPLICATION: FINANCIAL PROVISION AND PROPERTY ADJUSTMENT

Ancillary relief defined

3.1 The term 'ancillary relief', for the purposes of the Family Proceedings Rules 1991, is as follows[1]:

– avoidance of disposition orders;
– orders for financial provision[2];
– orders for maintenance pending suit;
– property adjustment orders;
– variation orders;
– orders for financial provision for children.

3.2 To this list, for the purposes of the Scheme, should be added applications[3] for consideration of her financial position by a respondent to a petition based on the facts of five years living apart or two years apart with consent under the Matrimonial Causes Act 1973, s 10(2) (a 'section 10(2) application') .

3.3 In this Chapter, only applications for financial provision or a property adjustment order will be considered. Applications for the remaining orders will be considered in Chapter 7. A Procedural Guide which summarises the operation of the Scheme is set out in Appendix 1.

The application

3.4 Under existing procedures, an application for ancillary relief is made in the petition or answer (if any) with a separate application (Form M13) to set the proceedings in motion; or it is commenced by an originating application in the matrimonial proceedings (Form M11)[4]. The Scheme harmonises these two, slightly different, procedures and provides that both processes be commenced by 'notice in Form A in Appendix 1A'[5]; although

---

1 Rule 1.2(1).

2 The definition in r 1.2(1) specifically excludes orders under the Matrimonial Causes Act 1973, s 27 (neglect to maintain).

3 Referred to in the amendment rules as 'an application to which Rule 2.45 applies' (see eg r 2.72(3)).

4 Family Proceedings Rules 1991, rr 2.53(1) and 2.58(1) (applications in petition or answer) and r 2.53(2) (all other applications).

5 Ibid, r 2.72(1).

applications should still be included in the petition or answer[6]. Where a pension adjustment order is sought its specific terms must be included in the application[7]. A section 10(2) application is made in Form B[8].

Issue and service

3.5   Upon the filing of Form A or Form B the court fixes a first appointment between 10 and 14 weeks from the date of filing and returns notice in Form C with details of the date of the first appointment[9]. The applicant then arranges service[10]. How service is effected will depend on the nature of the application, the form of property sought to be adjusted and whether or not there is a charge on that property[11]; and, save in the case of a respondent who has unencumbered freehold property (not common nowadays), the procedure for service is not clear. A suggestion for the principles which apply is as follows.

Respondent to the application

3.6   The respondent to an application is to be served 'within 4 [*sic*] days[12] of the date of filing of the notice'[13]. Thus far the provision is simple (save for problems over computation of time); but when the applicant considers exactly what must be served at this stage he finds that the rule states only that

---

6 Family Proceedings Rules 1991, r 2.72(1)(a). If an application is not included in the petition it can be made with leave in Form A pursuant to r 2.53(2)(a).

7 Ibid, r 2.72(2).

8 Ibid, r 2.72(3).

9 This is not what the rule says, but this process is suggested by the way the Scheme operates in practice and accounts for Form C (not otherwise referred to in the rules) in App 1A.

10 Good service of applications is dealt with in the Family Proceedings Rules 1991, rr 10.2 et seq, especially r 10.2(1) which provides for service on solicitors on the court record by first-class post, DX or fax, and (r 10.3(1)) by post to a person acting in person (although not, it seems, by fax – even if he has one).

11 It also depends on whether the application is for avoidance of disposition, for which see **8.8** below.

12 Time is computed in accordance with the Family Proceedings Rules 1991, r 1.5: eg in the computation of periods of less than seven days, days which are not 'business days' are ignored.

13 This is an unfortunate provision. It is accepted that it is probably based on the Family Proceedings Rules 1991, r 2.58; but that does no longer depend, in practice, on the court endorsing a date on a document alongside the application; and it is probably based on county court practice which involves the court in service of originating processes. It is to be hoped that this problem will be rectified on re-evaluation of these rules:

    (1) the solicitor responsible for service of the application has no control over the time which the court takes to issue or to return to him the application, so that if a week passes (ie only four working days plus a day for post) then the solicitor is already out of time for service which, given the emphasis on time constraints in the rules, might be taken against him;

    (2) that said, there is no means for either the applicant (who must compute the four days) or the respondent to know from Form C (as now drafted) on what date the application is treated by the court as filed.

he must 'serve a copy'[14]; but of what? It has become clear to practitioners who work under the Scheme that this means a copy of each of two documents: Form A and Form C (completed by the court with the date of the first appointment). These documents give the respondent notice of the application and of the date of the first appointment.

Mortgagees

3.7 Family Proceedings Rules 1991, r 2.59(2) and (4) have not been disapplied by the amendment rules and therefore they apply to applications under the Scheme. Form A[15] must include reference to 'any mortgage of the land [subject to a property adjustment order application] or any interest therein'[16]. Form A must then be served on the mortgagee; but when? The rules do not specify. The mortgagee can call for 'a copy of the applicant's affidavit' within 14 days of service; under the Scheme the nearest equivalent to that affidavit will be Form E which may not be filed until seven weeks before the first appointment. One might conclude, therefore, that service of Form A on mortgagees should coincide with the filing of Form E.

Trustees and settlors

3.8 As in the case of mortgagees, the Family Proceedings Rules 1991, r 2.59(3) has not been disapplied. It therefore applies to applications under the Scheme. Accordingly, Form A must be served on 'the trustees of [any settlement sought to be varied] and the settlor if living'. Time of service is not specified. In the case of trustees and settlors, service of Form A must be accompanied by 'a copy of the supporting affidavit'[17]. On the assumption that Form E can be treated as the affidavit in support, then service on trustees will need to await the filing of Form E.

Avoidance of disposition applications

3.9 Similar questions arise, in theory, in relation to trustees (above) as to disponees in relation to applications for avoidance of disposition; but in practice, because of its urgent nature, the procedure is bound to be very different[18].

Trustees or managers of a pension scheme

3.10 Similar provisions apply for trustees or managers of a pension scheme as for mortgagees, where application is made for an order which, as a result of the Matrimonial Causes Act 1973, ss 25B or 25C, will impose upon them any requirements as managers or trustees of the scheme. No order can be

---

14 Family Proceedings Rules 1991, 2.72(4)(b).
15 References to Forms M11 and M13 are to be treated as applications to Form A: Family Proceedings Rules 1991, r 2.71(3)(f).
16 Family Proceedings Rules 1991, r 2.59(2)(b).
17 Ie Form E: see under *Mortgagees* above.
18 See **8.5** et seq below.

made under ss 25B or 25C 'unless such provision has been sought by way of [Form A]¹⁹'. Form A must then be served on the trustee or manager. Since the trustee or manager can require the applicant 'to provide them with a copy of the affidavit supporting his application' within 14 days of service²⁰, since the nearest equivalent to that affidavit will be Form E and since that may not be filed until seven weeks before the first appointment, perhaps service of Form A should be geared to the filing of Form E.

STATEMENT IN FORM E

3.11   The statement in Form E is the document in which both parties set out their financial circumstances. The Family Proceedings Rules 1991, Part IV (proceedings under Children Act 1989) prescribes forms of application; but the evidence in support of that application is unrestricted as to extent, save by the usual rules, as to admissibility, and of evidence generally. By contrast, Form E and the Family Proceedings Rules 1991, r 2.73(2) (which defines the contents of the form) seek to restrict the extent to which each party sets out its evidence²¹; whilst r 2.73(3) seeks specifically to restrict discovery.

Limitations on discovery

3.12   Before considering Form E, it is appropriate to consider the question of discovery under the Scheme. Time and again, judges have been critical of the extent to which parties indulge in excessive discovery or their advisers are unable to restrain the incontinence of their disclosure. Rules already exist which, when used by the courts, can curb these excesses: from wasted costs orders²², through restrictions on taxation of costs²³, to a variety of

---

19 Family Proceedings Rules 1991, r 2.70(3) as amended by r 2.71(3)(f).

20 Ibid, r 2.70(5).

21 For the extent to which the rule as drawn can restrict the extent of evidence which a party can call: see **4.15** below.

22 Supreme Court Act 1981, s 51(7) and Rules of the Supreme Court 1965, Ord 62, r 11 as explained by *Ridehalgh v Horsefield* [1994] Ch 205, [1994] 2 FLR 194, CA; and see *Practice Direction of 31 January 1995 (Case Management)* [1995] 1 FLR 456, [1995] 1 WLR 332 at para 5.

23 See eg *G v G (Periodical Payments: Jurisdiction)* [1997] 1 FLR 368, CA per Ward LJ at 383E (at the conclusion of his judgment concerning an appeal on an application for variation of periodical payments): 'We were presented with a cardboard carton of six arch-lever files containing about 1200 pages of material totally irrelevant on this appeal, including bank statements and the myriad of other financial documents which burdened the district judge's inquiry. Such copying represented a total waste. It would seem to be in breach of the [rules] which direct solicitors how to prepare bundles for the Court of Appeal. It is now time that practitioners take note of . . . the taxing master's powers to disallow costs of unnecessary copying'.

practice directions[24]. What the Scheme seeks to do, as part of its aim to 'provide the court with much greater control over the conduct of proceedings than exists at present'[25], is to prevent discovery save where documents accompany Form E or as directed by the district judge[26].

Form E – the document

3.13 Form E is intended, in the main, to replace the affidavit of means, to limit disclosure to the factors set out in r 2.73(2) and to form a first step – often the main or only step – in providing the court with the information it needs to exercise its discretion under the Matrimonial Causes Act 1973, s 25, that is 'all the circumstances of the case' and 'in particular'[27] the factors set out in s 25(2). By the use of the words 'in particular' it is clear, therefore, that the legislature intended the list to be illustrative only of the main factors to be considered: not all factors are relevant to each case and 'all the circumstances' means that other factors outside the list can be considered.

3.14 Form E is described as 'a statement' but it is, in effect, an affidavit: it is signed and sworn by the spouse who makes the statement; and it contains certain prescribed information[28]. However, it differs radically from an affidavit of means. In an affidavit of means, subject to rules of evidence and, in particular, the rules relating to admissibility of relevant evidence, a deponent sets out facts and claims more or less at will. By contrast, the Scheme seeks to dictate to a party what information is to be provided. First, the Family Proceedings Rules 1991, r 2.73(2) sets out what is required to be included at this stage of the proceedings; and, secondly, a document for providing this information (Form E) is prescribed[29]. It is therefore important, when completing Form E, to ensure that what is in the form is indeed what is required by r 2.73(2). If not, it is submitted, the rule takes precedence over the form, where the two are inconsistent; and information required by the form need not be included as a party wishes. The requirements of the rule are that a variety of information be given. The following factors in the list of information require comment:

---

24 [Vive moi] See eg *Practice Direction of 31 January 1995 (Case Management)* [1995] 1 FLR 456, [1995] 1 WLR 332 at paras 2(a) (power of court to limit discovery), 4(a) (duty of legal representatives to confine evidence to what is reasonably essential) and 5 (disallowance of costs for incompetent preparation of bundles); *B v B (Court Bundles: Video Evidence)* [1994] 2 FLR 323, Wall J – Practice Note, especially para 10 concerning 'rigorous pruning of unnecessary material'.
25 *President's Direction of 25 July 1996* at para 1.
26 Family Proceedings Rules 1991, rr 2.73(3)(a) and (4)(b) and 2.74(1)(a)(ii).
27 Matrimonial Causes Act 1973, s 25(1) and (2).
28 Ibid, r 2.73(1).
29 Ibid, r 2.73(1) and App 1A.

'(b) the party's state of health'

3.15   Form E requires, in addition to the party's state of health, details of 'the state of health of . . . the children'. Section 25(2)(e) requires the court only to have regard to 'any physical or mental disability' of the parties. Reference to this occurs at 4(e) of the Form. It is difficult to see how the court is assisted by knowledge of a party's state of health beyond the requirements of s 25(2)(e).

'(f) a concise statement of the party's means'

3.16   In principle, this equates to 'property and other financial resources' in the Matrimonial Causes Act 1973, s 25(2)(a) and the value of any benefit which a 'party will lose the chance of acquiring' as a result of dissolution of the marriage under s 25(2)(h). However, Form E veers dramatically away from the detail of r 2.72(2)(f) particularising as precisely as possible a variety of forms of asset which a party may hold. Cars are included[30], as are cash[31] and bank accounts[32].

'(f)(iii) Pensions'

3.17   Even – or especially – lay clients are aware that pensions or their transfer or any other value are not assets, properly so called. They are a contingent benefit with no realisable cash value. Accordingly, to include 'pension values' as part of the 'grand total of [a party's] net assets' or as a net asset[33] is confusing.

'(f)(iv) Insurance policies'

3.18   Rule 2.73(2)(f)(iv) requires details of date of maturity of insurance policies and their surrender value; but Form E[34] requires also the maturity value of the policy. On the face of it this is not unreasonable, but the form then asks for the 'value' of the policy which, according to one's interpretation of the boxes, could mean either surrender value or maturity value. Lawyers will realise that the form must refer to surrender value. Lay persons conducting their own applications may be confused by this ambiguity.

'(g) a concise statement of any loss of widow's or widower's pension'

3.19   Although this information is required by r 2.72(2)(g), no space is provided for it in Form E so, for the present, it may be left without comment – save for the hope that no party is criticised for not including this information in their statement of means.

---

30 Form E para 2(j).

31 Form E para 2(i). To the question as to 'where [the cash] is held', the answer from one client was, quite reasonably, 'in my hand bag'.

32 Form E para 2(c). Current accounts, which are no doubt required (in a form which seeks details of cash held), like many debts (eg credit card accounts) will be a moving target and may change between preparation of the form and its swearing. It should be explained to a client to give the best estimate only.

33 Grand total 'H' after 2 (p) and 'Summary of financial information' at the end of Part 2 of Form E.

34 Paragraph 2(e).

'(h) present and future reasonable needs'

3.20 This is a question which should only be answered with extreme care (if at all); or in terms which will be of limited value to the reader of Form E. Any lawyer who advises a client to state their needs before disclosure is complete[35] and property[36] is realistically valued, risks a negligence claim. The prudent answer here is that a party's needs are for a home and food and clothing, together with any special needs related to disability: the rest is a matter for argument when the parties' financial resources are fully known[37].

'(m) Conduct'

3.21 Given that the likelihood of the court taking conduct into account will be rare[38], and that there is a section devoted to 'any other circumstances'[39], it is unfortunate that 'conduct' should be given prominence in the way that it is, especially in Form E[40]. It may be difficult to persuade some spouses confronted with the encouragement provided by the form that the particular conduct of which they complain is irrelevant to the court's deliberations. The consequence of pleading conduct is that further particulars will be provided if the spouse wishes to rely on the allegation in financial relief proceedings[41].

Other factors

3.22 One of the difficulties of a document, such as Form E, is that the definition of significant terms can be overlooked by the draftsman. For example, Part 4 of the form uses the term 'your current spouse' (para 4(a)) whilst two boxes later the term 'your partner' (4(c)) appears. This will cause confusion especially since no reference to either of these is made in r 2.73(2).

(a) 'Current spouse' – given the context, this probably means the other party to proceedings.

---

35 *Dickenson v Jones, Alexander & Co* [1993] 2 FLR 521, Douglas Brown J (professional negligence claim against solicitors who advised acceptance of an offer from a husband who had not given full disclosure and who turned out to be very wealthy, quite unknown to his former wife): one wonders what Mrs Dickinson would have said in answer to this question.

36 See eg *B v Miller & Co* [1996] 2 FLR 23, McKinnon J (QBD) (wife accepted payment without valuation of the matrimonial home, which turned out to be worth much more than she or her legal advisers thought).

37 'The proper approach of the court should be to take the wife's reasonable requirements and balance those against the husband's ability to pay. That involves a general consideration of his sources of income and capital and, in particular, of his liquidity': *Potter v Potter* (1983) 4 FLR 331, CA per Dunne LJ at 334E; cited with approval by eg Anthony Lincoln J in *B v B (Financial Provision)* [1989] 1 FLR 119.

38 Reported cases are limited to rare circumstances.

39 Rule 2.72(2)(n) and Form E, para 4(e).

40 Paragraph 4(d).

41 *Practice Direction of 4 June 1981* [1981] 1 WLR 1010, para (d).

(b)   'Your partner' – this term has developed a special meaning in the past few years (outside the context of business partnership) implying a relationship between a man and a woman which falls short of marriage; but is that what Form E means? In the context – a partner who makes 'contributions to the family property and assets' – it is difficult to see why the sexual partner connotation should be assumed.

For both the present terms, the best advice would seem to be to make no attempt to answer para (a) and to ignore 'your partner' in para 4(c) and refer to r 2.73(2) if a district judge is critical.

Service and filing of Form E

3.23   Not less than five weeks before the first appointment, the completed Form E must be filed at court and exchanged 'simultaneously' with the other party[42]. Some practitioners may insist on exchange being precisely simultaneous; but, save for those concerned excessively with some form of tactical advantage, an exchange which is literally simultaneous hardly seems necessary. In providing for simultaneous exchange, perhaps the draftsman of the rule was concerned to get away from the filing of affidavits on a sequential basis as is required by the existing procedure[43].

---

42 Family Proceedings Rules 1991, r 2.73(1).
43 Ibid, r 2.58(2) and (3).

Chapter 4

THE FIRST APPOINTMENT

'OBJECTIVES' OF THE FIRST APPOINTMENT

4.1 The first appointment is intended to be conducted by the district judge 'with the objective of defining the issues and saving costs'[1]. To this end, prior to the hearing, the parties file and serve on each other requests for further information and documents, a statement of the issues in the case[2] and produce at court on the day of the appointment a written estimate of costs[3]. The district judge then gives directions for the future conduct of proceedings. The bases on which these directions are to be given are defined by the rules[4]. This has not hitherto been the case in ancillary relief proceedings since under the existing rules the giving of directions 'as to the further conduct of proceedings' is discretionary[5]. It will be recalled that 'no discovery of documents [may] be sought or given' save those annexed to Form E[6].

BEFORE THE FIRST APPOINTMENT

4.2 As the first appointment approaches the parties will have exchanged Form E. Thus each will know what the other is saying about their means and what they are seeking by way of court order. Under the existing procedures, upon a party filing an affidavit, the other may seek further relevant information or documents by letter[7]. If that request is not complied with, a court order for reply can be applied for from the district judge. Thus the district judge becomes involved in the process only if replies are not given, or documents not provided. By contrast, under the Scheme, the intention is that the district judge should keep much more control of this process.

---

1 Family Proceedings Rules 1991, r 2.74(1). This concept of an 'objective' represents a novel development in family law jurisprudence akin to the Family Law Act 1996, where the legislature superimposes an aspiration or general principle on an aspect of the law.

2 Ibid, r 2.73(4).

3 Ibid, r 2.76.

4 Ibid, r 2.74(1).

5 Ibid, r 2.62(5).

6 Ibid, r 2.72(3).

7 Ibid, r 2.63. The rule specifies a 'letter', although in practice the request is normally by more formal questionnaire. This rule has been disapplied under the Scheme: see **2.5** above.

Accordingly, not later than seven days[8] before the first appointment, each party must file their requests for information and documents. In addition, the parties are required at this stage to give their assessment of the issues in the case, since admissibility of evidence depends upon its relevance to the issues before the court, 'and all [evidence] that is irrelevant, or insufficiently relevant, should be excluded'[9].

Questionnaire seeking further information and schedule seeking documents

4.3 A problem with a system which directs the filing of a questionnaire and schedule[10] (as distinct from making it permissive, as under the Family Proceedings Rules 1991, r 2.63) is that parties may feel obliged to ask questions where in fact there may be no questions of significance to raise, or to seek documents where there are none to request or none which are needed. Where a questionnaire or request for documents is to be drafted, the following should be borne in mind:

(a)   *Relevance to issues* – requests for information and documents must be relevant to the issues in the case.

(b)   *Oppressive questions* – questions must not be oppressive[11] in the sense of being particularly difficult or needlessly expensive to answer.

(c)   *Questions and directions* – there is no need to ask as a question that which can be dealt with by directions at court (eg as to the filing of opinion evidence from an actuary) or in correspondence between the parties (eg as to whether valuation evidence is agreed).

(d)   *Cross-examination at the final hearing* – the other party will be at court to be cross-examined at the final hearing. It is desirable to elicit as many facts as possible before the hearing, but where he or she will not answer, or where it is not facts which are wanted (eg intentions for the future), it may be necessary to await the final hearing for certain information.

---

8 This is not the same as a week, since days which are not 'business days' are excluded, in respect of periods of less than seven days; and neither the date on which, nor the date by which, the act is to be done count towards the period: Family Proceedings Rules 1991, r 1.5(2) and (4). Thus, if the first appointment falls on a Wednesday, proper compliance with r 2.73(4) would involve serving and filing the documents not later than the Friday nearly two weeks before. It is doubtful whether this is what the draftsman of the rule intended (see eg the Commentary, para 3 under 'The Third Part').

9 *Cross & Tapper on Evidence* 8th Edn (Butterworths, 1995) at p 56.

10 Family Proceedings Rules 1991, r 2.73(4) is mandatory, where perhaps (a) and (b) could have been permissive and the remainder of the sub-rule mandatory.

11 See further **4.15** below.

A concise statement of the issues between the parties

4.4 'The issues between the parties' is not a term which is defined by the amendment rules. For the experienced advocate the meaning will be clear. In defining what is meant by 'the issues between the parties' the following should be taken into consideration:

(a)   The classic definition of the issues is those matters for decision by the court to be distilled from the pleadings. For the lawyer dealing with ancillary relief under the Scheme the only pleading, properly so called, is Form A. Form E is evidence; although there is no doubt that it is from Form E that the issues between the parties are to be deduced.

(b)   In most civil and criminal proceedings the evidence is in the past and the issues are therefore static: that is to say the facts on which the prosecution base their case or the plaintiff bases his claim in tort have happened. In family cases, especially children cases, the issues can often be dynamic[12]: they are happening as the case proceeds; or they may emerge with discovery. It is not always easy, therefore, to state the issues with too much certainty long in advance of the final hearing.

(c)   That said, an attempt must be made to define the issues: not only to satisfy r 2.73(4)(c), but also the better to be able to define the relevance of evidence – the extent to which questionnaries are to be answered and documents ordered to be disclosed.

'The issues' – a definition

4.5   Issues fall into two main categories:

(a)   Primary issues – issues for resolution by the court by court order; and
(b)   Secondary, or evidential, issues – issues on the evidence on which the court may or may not need to make a finding in order to resolve one or more of the primary issues.

(a) Primary issues

4.6   A primary issue will be a question on which the court can make an order[13]; for example:

–   whether or not the former matrimonial home should be sold;
–   if sold, in what proportions should the proceeds be divided;
–   if not sold (so that the wife stays in the house), whether there should be a charge-back in favour of the husband;
–   whether the wife should have periodical payments;
–   if so, how much, for how long and should there be an order under the Matrimonial Causes Act 1973 s 28(1A);
–   whether there should be a clean break.

---

12   See consideration of this question by Burrows and Parker at [1993] Fam Law 156.
13   Note the reminder in *Dinch v Dinch* [1987] 2 FLR 162, [1987] 1 WLR 252, HL that the court can only make orders in accordance with its powers under the Matrimonial Causes Act 1973.

(b) Secondary, or evidential, issues

4.7   Evidential issues surrounding the above primary issues might include:

–   the availability of alternative property which the wife could buy;

–   the extent to which the wife is or is not realising her earning capacity;

–   the husband's need for capital (and perhaps he is living with a woman who has property: a particularly difficult evidential issue);

–   the extent to which both have other assets and either has a pension fund (for definition of quantum of the charge-back or lump sums, if a sale is ordered).

'A concise statement of the issues'

4.8   The primary issues are those which the court will require to have set out in the statement for the purposes of r 2.73(4)(c): that is to say, the aspects of the case on which a district judge can assist with mediation or on which he is able to make an order (as distinct from making findings on the evidence) if the case goes to a final hearing. It is on these secondary issues that the district judge will then, most likely, be involved in giving directions (see Example below). The advocate who attends the first appointment will need to have these secondary issues in mind; but they need not necessarily included in the statement of issues.

> **Example**
>
> Mr and Mrs Cromwell: their circumstances on the day of the first appointment:
>
> Anne Cromwell ('W' aged 27) and Tom Cromwell ('H' aged 39) were married six years ago and lived together at 32 Essex Court, a house which is owned by them jointly and on which there is a mortgage of £67,000. H left some 18 months ago. They have one child Mary (aged 4). W is a trained teacher, but is not now working. H is the director and sole shareholder of a company which he set up some years ago.
>
> When he left the former matrimonial home, H went to live with Mrs Parr. She is well-off in her own right, but they have had drawn up by her solicitors a cohabitation agreement under which it is agreed by them that they have no claim on each other's capital assets and that H should pay a set sum to Mrs Parr as board and lodging and as his contribution to the expenses of her household. W has an association with John Colet, a man much younger than her, whose only visible means of support is from part-time teaching: he is not, so far, making his way in his chosen profession of poet. H says W and Colet are living together.
>
> H's pension fund has a transfer value of £83,000; whilst the value of W's fund is negligible. Neither have any other assets. H has over £8,000 in credit card debts and owes the last term's school fees for Mary at her private infant school.
>
> The value of the house is not agreed; nor are the value of H's shares in his business.

Primary issues

(1)   Whether or not H should have a lump sum from the house, and in consequence whether the house should be sold[14].

(2)   If the house were to be sold, what lump sum should each spouse have: proportions or one having a set amount with the balance to the other?

(3)   If the house is not to be sold:

    (a)   Should H pay any lump sum to W in addition to her share in the house?

    (b)   Should H have an interest in the former matrimonial home either by way of share or charge-back; and if so on what terms as to time for sale or repayment of charge?

(4)   Is W entitled to any earmarking of H's pension: if so, how much; or is this a case where there are sufficient assets for that to be unnecessary.

(5)   What quantum of periodical payments should she have for herself: (a) if she stays in the house; (b) if she does not?

(6)   Should there be a s 28(1A) cut-off on these payments; and if so, when?

Secondary (evidential) issues

(1)   Value of former matrimonial home.

(2)   H's liquidity (probably the value of his business will be irrelevant).

(3)   W's earning capacity.

(4)   Property to which W can move.

(5)   The needs of the child to continue to live in the family home.

(6)   Amount of child support maintenance (if not agreed).

(7)   Relevance of H's admitted cohabitation and extent (if any) of W's cohabitation.

Confirmation of service on mortgagees, trustees, pension trustees and others

4.9   Where rules require service of mortgagees, trustees, settlors, disponees of land where avoidance of disposition is sought, or pension adjustment orders where a requirement is imposed on pension fund trustees or managers, then confirmation that these individuals or bodies concerned have been served in accordance with the rules[15] must be produced at court and served on the other party.

Costs

4.10   At every hearing, each party (where they are represented) must produce to the court an 'estimate of the solicitor and own client costs' incurred to the date of hearing. Solicitor and own client costs are essentially costs which are taxed on the indemnity basis[16] and approved by the client or

---

14   An order for sale under the Matrimonial Causes Act 1973, s 24A can be made only if a triggering order is made, the most appropriate order here being (for H) a lump sum order.

15   For the bodies concerned and questions over arrangements for service, see **3.7** et seq above.

16   Rules of the Supreme Court 1965, Ord 62, r 12(2); and see *F v F (Duxbury Calculation: Rate of Return)* [1996] 1 FLR 833, Holman J for further explanation of 'indemnity basis'.

impliedly approved by him[17]. Solicitor and own client costs do not apply in respect of a bill taxed under the Civil Legal Aid (General) Regulations 1989, SI 1989/339[18]. Thus in calculating a bill for the purposes of this rule the advocate should prepare it on the basis of it being charged to the other party on an indemnity basis.

THE APPOINTMENT

Purpose of directions

4.11   One of the more striking aspects of the Family Proceedings Rules 1991, r 2.75(1), which deals with directions at the first hearing, is that it is written in mandatory terms; save for the final sub-paragraph dealing with interim orders, adjournment for an FDR and notice to pension trustees. The district judge must therefore go through a list of requirements set out in the rule which may have the disappointing result of reducing judicial discretion in an area of law hitherto generally noted for the breadth of discretion available to the courts.

4.12   The object of directions is to ensure that a case is ready for trial. A secondary object is to prepare the ground for financial dispute resolution, if this appears possible in the particular case. In either instance, this will ensure that disclosure is as complete as is reasonably possible and that all evidence, relevant to the issues before the court, is available for the hearing. Under existing procedures, disclosure and the marshalling of evidence are left entirely to the parties, subject to any request they may make for directions or orders on the subject[19]. The extent to which district judges will now become involved in seeking to indicate what additional evidence they wish to have called to enable them to exercise their discretion remains to be seen; for, as a general rule, they cannot refuse to hear admissible evidence.

Evidence generally

The questionnaire
4.13   Where a questionnaire has been filed and served the district judge will be concerned to 'determine ... the extent to which [it] shall be answered'[20]. There has been considerable concern[21] at the extent to which parties have over-extended their questionnaires. The Scheme should change nothing in

---

17 Rules of the Supreme Court 1965, Ord 62, r 15(2).
18 Ibid, Ord 62, r 15(1).
19 See eg Family Proceedings Rules 1991, r 2.63 (requests for further information and documents), Rules of the Supreme Court 1965, Ords 24 (discovery) and 26 (interrogatories).
20 Family Proceedings Rules 1991, r 2.74(a)(i).
21 See eg the Commentary, paras 1 and 3 on 'Steps 6–8&11'.

this respect: the questions remain the same. The problem under the existing procedure is that practitioners feel unable to resist answering questions which they should have refused to answer (because the questions were irrelevant to the issues or because they were oppressive). The district judges can now refuse to require a question to be answered, *in limine*; so the doubts as to whether a question need be answered will no longer exist. It is possible, under the Scheme,[22] that questionnaires may be encouraged where none might previously have been raised.

4.14 As to the criteria for ordering a response, they remain the same as hitherto: whether or not the answer to the question is likely to be relevant, or sufficiently relevant, to the issues before the court. It is a matter for the court's discretion as to whether it orders the answer[23]; and it should not do so if it would be oppressive of a witness[24]. If a party presses for information, the court can order that, if the replies prove to be irrelevant, the cost of providing them should fall on that party[25].

Evidence generally

4.15 At the first appointment the district judge 'shall give directions as to (iii) any evidence sought to be adduced by each party'[26]. It is not yet known how this provision is intended to be used. However, there should be no doubt that the court's powers – if they exist at all[27] – to refuse to hear relevant evidence are very limited indeed; provided only that, in cases dealt with on affidavit, an affidavit[28] is sworn by the witness whose evidence the party wishes to have available before the court. Further, it should be borne in mind that the evidence put forward in Form E is limited by the form. In some cases, especially where some explanation as to the history of a marriage, or of a person's present financial state (whether good or bad), is relevant, then a further affidavit by a party will be relevant. It would seem prudent to give notice at a directions appointment that such evidence is to be called and to seek from the district judge a direction as to when it is to be filed.

Documentary evidence: discovery

4.16 The district judge next considers the extent to which 'documents requested under Rule 2.73[(4)(b)] shall be produced and give directions

---

22 As already mentioned at **4.3** above.
23 In giving directions the court will bear in mind the frequent judicial criticism of over-enquiry: see eg *Attar v Attar* [1985] FLR 649, Booth J; *B v B (Financial Provision)* [1989] 1 FLR 119, Anthony Lincoln J.
24 Perhaps on analogy with the Rules of the Supreme Court 1965, Ord 26, r 1 (interrogatories); and see *Hildebrand v Hildebrand* [1992] 1 FLR 244, Waite J.
25 *Practice Direction* [1981] 1 WLR 1010, [1981] 2 All ER 642.
26 Family Proceedings Rules 1991, r 2.74(1)(b)(iii).
27 See further **6.3** below.
28 In the case of opinion evidence, witness evidence will normally be before the court in the form of a report, and subject to the provisions of Ord 38, r 36: see **4.18** et seq below.

for the production of such further documents as may be necessary'. The normal rule in ancillary relief cases is that parties are required to give full relevant disclosure of information relating to their application[29] (which in cases dealt with on affidavit frequently means discovering[30] documents in support: ie exhibiting them to an affidavit) and the other party may then seek discovery[31]. Under the Scheme, the object is to limit inter partes discovery[32] only:

(a)   to what is necessarily annexed to Form E; and
(b)   to such documents as may be directed to be disclosed by the district judge.

It is thus a matter for the district judge's discretion as to what is disclosed; and this discretion will be exercised upon the same bases as for evidence generally[33].

4.17   In particular, it will be noted that the district judge specifically has a duty to direct production of such other documents 'as may be necessary'. This will involve the district judge, at the directions stage, in considering what documents will be required for the exercise of the court's discretion at any final hearing.

Valuation evidence

4.18   Rule 2.74(1)(b)(i) and (ii) requires the district judge to give directions as to valuations and expert evidence. The extent to which opinion evidence may be called – save where it is agreed by the parties – has always been a matter for the court; for the expert witness is there to assist the court first, the parties second. The object of expert evidence is that the expert should assist the court impartially in areas where the judge is not expected to be knowledgeable. This rule has been explained recently by Ward LJ thus: 'The court has no expertise of its own, other than legal expertise ... The expert advises, but the judge decides'[34]. From this it follows that if the expert is seeking to give opinion evidence on a matter on which the court already has expertise (eg some aspect of accountancy), the court would be entitled to exclude the evidence.

4.19   The Rules of the Supreme Court 1965, Ord 38, rr 34–43 and the

---

29 *Jenkins v Livesey (formerly Jenkins)* [1985] AC 424, sub nom *Livesey (formerly Jenkins) v Jenkins* [1985] FLR 813, HL.
30 In the technical sense of the term: literally lifting the cover off.
31 In civil cases generally, there is a duty to give discovery by lists (Rules of the Supreme Court 1965, Ord 24, r 5). The recipient of the list may then seek discovery of further documents which are thought not to have been disclosed. In ancillary relief cases, this procedure is normally now limited to the procedure under the Family Proceedings Rules 1991, r 2.63 (but see *Re JC (Care Proceedings: Procedure)* [1995] 2 FLR 77, Wall J for seeking documents by discovery under Ord 24 in children proceedings).
32 Family Proceedings Rules 1991, r 2.73(3).
33 See **4.14** above, especially fnn 25 and 26.
34 *Re B (Care: Expert Witness)* [1996] 1 FLR 667, CA at 670C–D.

County Court Rules 1981, Ord 20, rr 25–28 provide the procedural structure for opinion and expert evidence; and there is nothing in r 2.74(1) which suggests that the courts should depart from Ord 38. (In what follows, reference will be made only to Ord 38 since Ord 20 effectively adopts it in its entirety for proceedings in the county courts). The Scheme specifically implies 'joint instruction of independent experts'[35]; an object of the Scheme is to save costs; and there is recent evidence of judicial approval of appointment of a court expert[36].

Leave or agreement to adduce expert evidence

4.20   An essential feature of expert evidence is the requirement of fairness and mutuality between the parties; for the party who is unable to respond to the opinion of an expert, because he does not know of the opinion in advance of the hearing, may be prejudiced. The rules reflect this by providing that expert evidence cannot be adduced save:

(a)   by leave of the court;
(b)   by agreement of the parties;
(c)   by affidavit in appropriate circumstances; or
(d)   in accordance with court directions[37].

The Scheme reflects this by providing for directions (rather than leave) for the adducing of expert evidence.

Meeting of experts

4.21   The court, of its own motion, may 'direct that there be a meeting "without prejudice"' of experts involved in the case, 'for the purpose of identifying the parts of their evidence which are in issue'[38]. They may then produce a joint statement identifying points agreed and any points which remain in issue. This concept has been clearly reproduced in r 2.74(1)(b) (i), and it is likely that district judges will be keen to use it, especially on questions of valuation where a telephone conversation between two valuers may resolve their differences and produce an agreed value.

---

35 Family Proceedings Rules 1991, r 2.74(1)(b)(i).
36 Appointed under Rules of the Supreme Court 1965, Ord 40 (even though at present this provision may only be available in the High Court); and see *Re K (Psychiatric Report)* [1995] 2 FLR 432, CA and *Abbey National Mortgagees plc v Key Surveyors Nationwide Ltd and Others* [1996] 1 WLR 1534, CA.
37 Rules of the Supreme Court 1965, Ord 38, r 36; County Court Rules 1981, Ord 20, r 27.
38 Rules of the Supreme Court 1965, Ord 38, r 38; and see approval of this procedure in *Access to Justice: Final Report* by Lord Woolf MR, (HMSO, July 1996) Ch 13, para 42 et seq.

Report disclosed by another party

4.22 A party is entitled to put in as part of his own evidence any report disclosed by another party[39]. It would then be the responsibility of the party using a report in that way to call the expert at the hearing if wishing to rely on his evidence.

Court experts

4.23 The High Court may appoint an expert 'on the application of any party' to the proceedings before the court[40]. The function of the expert is 'to inquire and report upon any question of fact or opinion not involving questions of law or of construction'[41]. If possible, he should be a person agreed between the parties and the question to be put to him should be agreed between them, failing which the court will appoint and settle instructions to him[42]. His report is sent to the court and then to the parties who, if they wish to cross-examine him, must seek leave[43]. The court fixes his fee which is payable by the parties who are jointly and severally liable for it subject to any order for costs the court may make in the cause or application[44]. With notice to other parties a party may call evidence on the question to be reported on to the court, for which there appears to be no requirement for leave[45].

4.24 Support for a scheme along the lines of Ord 40 but operated by the court on its own motion is advocated by Lord Woolf MR[46]; and Sir Thomas Bingham MR has upheld a 'novel' direction under Ord 40[47] upon the following bases:

– 'exhortations to trial judges[48] to be interventionist and managerial' should be heeded by making orders of this sort; whilst the court must 'be constantly alert to the paramount requirements of justice' to both parties (at 1537B–C);

– to avoid the 'fact' that expert witnesses, if called by a party, tend 'to espouse the cause of those instructing them'; whilst a court-appointed expert may, by contrast, 'prove a reliable source of expert opinion' (at 1542B–C); and

---

39 Rules of the Supreme Court 1965, Ord 38, r 42.
40 Ibid, Ord 40, r 1(1). There is no equivalent rule in the county courts.
41 Ibid, Ord 40, r 1(1).
42 Ibid, Ord 40, r 1(2) and (3).
43 Ibid, Ord 40, r 4.
44 Ibid, Ord 40, r 5.
45 Ibid, Ord 40, r 6; although, where applicable, an issue might arise on costs, especially where a party has agreed the expert and his terms of reference.
46 *Access to Justice: Final Report* by Lord Woolf MR, (HMSO, July 1996) Ch 13, para 16 et seq.
47 *Abbey National Mortgagees Plc v Key Surveyors Nationwide Ltd and Others* (above).
48 Ie in case management practice directions such as, in the Family Division, *Practice Direction of 31 January 1995 (Case Management)* [1995] 1 FLR 456, [1995] 1 WLR 332.

– regard for the costs, relative to the values of the properties concerned, of giving leave to each party to adduce the evidence of individual experts in each case (at 1542F).

Although *Abbey National v Keys* (above) was a case involving a large number of properties, the principles set out by the Master of the Rolls would seem as applicable to the objectives of the Scheme. It remains only to hope that before long the court expert can be appointed in the county court.

'Chronologies or schedules'

4.25 A problem with compiling a chronology from Form E will be that a number of the items for inclusion will not be available from the Forms which will by this time have been exchanged[49]; and yet a chronology should be based only on evidence available to the court. The advocate will need to decide whether to prepare an affidavit which includes the points which are intended to be in the chronology or to include matters in the chronology which are either capable of agreement or which, if challenged, can be clarified by examination-in-chief. This last would be unfortunate; for the essence of a chronology should be that it states facts impartially.

Referral to an FDR appointment

4.26 Unless he considers it inappropriate in the circumstances of the particular case, the district judge must direct that the application be 'referred to' an FDR appointment[50]. At this point the application can go in one of four directions:

(1) the district judge may treat the first appointment as the FDR;
(2) a further directions appointment may be fixed;
(3) directions may be given for the final hearing; or
(4) the application may be adjourned to an FDR appointment.

(1) First appointment as FDR

4.27 'With the consent of both parties' the district judge can treat the first appointment as an FDR appointment[51]. Where the district judge has fully considered Form E, where the issues are well defined and where outstanding questions and documents seem to him unlikley to reveal a great deal more about the case, he can proceed to consider prospects for settlement. If settlement cannot then be achieved, it will enable the court to move immediately to the final hearing, subject to directions as to answering of questionnaires, the provision of documents and any other outstanding matters being dealt with. Dealing with the first appointment in this way will

---

49 Or if they are all there what is the purpose of a chronology?
50 Family Proceedings Rules 1991, r 2.74(1)(c).
51 Ibid, r 2.74(1)(f)(ii); and see further Ch 5.

unquestionably be in accordance with an object of the first appointment and of the Scheme as a whole: namely the 'saving [of] costs'[52].

If the FDR aspect of the appointment fails the district judge can give directions for a final hearing as at (3) below.

(2) Further directions

4.28   Where the application is not ready, even for an FDR, the court will adjourn for further directions[53]: for example, so that valuation evidence can be clarified, further documents obtained and analysed or further evidence obtained where the time for obtaining it is uncertain. In only 'exceptional circumstances' may the court adjourn the application generally[54]; and given the tenor of r 2.72(5)[55], it seems likely that such circumstances will have to be truly exceptional.

(3) Directions for a final hearing

4.29   If directions for a final hearing are given – either because the case is not thought suitable for FDR or the first appointment has been treated as an FDR which has not resulted in settlement – the district judge will determine at what level of judge the case should be heard. Under the existing procedure, cases are heard by the district judge[56] unless referred by the district judge 'to a judge for his decision'[57]. The presumption is therefore that a district judge will try every case, unless he directs otherwise. The likelihood is that this presumption will remain in practice, although this is not made clear by r 2.74(1)(d)(iii).

(4) Adjourn for FDR

4.30   There is a duty upon the district judge to refer the case for FDR, in default of which he must find that a referral is positively inappropriate[58].

(5) Adjourn for private mediation or negotiation

4.31   This provision enables the parties, effectively, to refer themselves for mediation privately or to continue negotiations by such means as they may choose (eg through their solicitors)[59]. This sub-rule reflects the Family Law Act 1996 (in which before marital order parties must settle their financial affairs by negotiation and the court can adjourn to make this possible). The implication of the drafting is that it is only in exceptional circumstances that

---

52 Family Proceedings Rules 1991, r 2.74(1).
53 Ibid, r 2.74(1)(d)(i).
54 Ibid, r 2.74(1)(d)(iv).
55 Once issued with a first appointment, that appointment cannot be adjourned without leave
    of the court and without another date being fixed.
56 Family Proceedings Rules 1991, r 2.62(4).
57 Ibid, r 2.65.
58 Ibid, r 2.74(1)(c). For consideration of the FDR see Ch 5.
59 Ibid, r 2.74(1)(d)(iv).

a case will be adjourned generally and that this does not include mediation or negotiation; so it seems likely that the court will adjourn to a date. If a case is to be adjourned for mediation, advocates should be sure to attend the appointment before the district judge with a reasonably clear idea of when mediation is likely to be concluded.

CONCLUSION

4.32 Three final matters need to be considered before moving to the FDR: further directions, attendance of the parties and their advocates, and costs. The question of interim orders is also one which arises in r 2.74(1); but this subject will be considered in Chapter 8[60].

Further directions

4.33 An option available to the district judge who decides referral to an FDR is inappropriate as the first appointment, is to adjourn for further directions[61]. This might be particularly apt in, for example, more complicated cases where further discovery, or further information, is needed[62] before a true assessment of the case can be made sufficient to enable a district judge to assess whether an FDR appointment could realistically be undertaken.

Attendance of the parties

4.34 Unless the court orders otherwise, both parties must attend the first appointment and any adjournment thereof[63]. Given the possibility of the court using the first appointment as an FDR, quite apart from the likelihood that at such a directions appointment as this most advocates will need the client's instructions on the spot, the reason for the Scheme's insistence on a party's attendance is unarguable. If a client is unavoidably unavailable, the court should be told immediately and the district judge asked to give leave for non-attendance of the client or to adjourn[64]; although it is likely that in most instances the court will adjourn to a date when both parties can be present in person. If a client is unable to attend court because of a disability, the court should be asked to fix the appointment at a place where the client can attend. Such application can be made in writing, accompanied by

---

60 See **8.3** below.

61 Family Proceedings Rules 1991, r 2.74(1)(d)(i).

62 If a party has needlessly caused the adjournment of the first appointment by inadequate disclosure, that party may be penalised in costs.

63 Family Proceedings Rules 1991, r 2.74(4).

64 This application, whatever the district judge's decision, seems likely to attract a fee of £20.

medical evidence in support, and with copy correspondence and reports being sent to the other party.

Costs

4.35   Concern for costs is a pervasive aspect of the Scheme[65], and the first appointment is no exception. The implication[66] is that if parties do not properly comply with what is required by the time of the first appointment – for example, a properly completed Form E or adequate summaries of issues – then they may be penalised. However, it is to be hoped that mere failure slavishly to follow the requirements for preparation will not attract an order: some prejudice to the other party must be shown.

Advocacy at the first, and further, appointments

4.36   The question of advocacy could probably not be provided for in the amendment rules, nor is it mentioned in the Commentary. However, it must be desirable, wherever possible, that the same advocate represents the client throughout the series of appointments leading up to and including the final hearing (if any). Certain courts which already have, or have had, pre-hearing arrangements similar to the Scheme have insisted that, where possible, the advocate who attends the pre-trial mediation appointment be the same as the advocate who is to deal with the final hearing[67]. This must be desirable from the client's point of view.

---

65 See further Ch 7.

66 See the Commentary, Step 10, para 6: 'the court may make an order for costs if lack of adherence to these rules warrants it'.

67 From this it follows that a further practical tip is that advocates should carry with them in some form a court diary – as most children lawyers do; for the likelihood is that district judges, as part of their directions, will adjourn the application to a date fixed specifically at the appointment.

Chapter 5

THE FINANCIAL DISPUTE RESOLUTION APPOINTMENT

5.1 The route to the Financial Dispute Resolution appointment ('FDR') is via the first appointment, either during the course of that appointment or following adjournment from it[1]. The only basis on which an FDR will not occur is because the district judge considers that referral for FDR is 'not appropriate in the circumstances' of the case.

5.2 Before an FDR can be effective there must be full relevant disclosure by both sides; for settlement without full disclosure leaves the party who does not disclose open to an application to set aside any order obtained[2] – whether by settlement of the case or following a contested hearing. Negotiations with a view to settlement are meaningless without full disclosure; just as a *Calderbank* letter cannot properly be so called until discovery has been given and disclosure is complete[3].

PREREQUISITES FOR A FINANCIAL DISPUTE RESOLUTION APPOINTMENT

5.3 For the FDR to be effective certain prerequisites are essential, and, in addition, the rules place certain other obligations on the parties:

(1)   all requirements as to disclosure must be complete;
(2)   *Calderbank* correspondence must be available to the court;
(3)   the applicant and respondent must attend court; and
(4)   the court must be provided with a costs estimate.

Requirements as to disclosure complete

5.4 Prior to the FDR it is essential, at the very least, that Form E be completed with the information required by the Family Proceedings Rules 1991, r 2.73(2)[4], that documents be provided, questionnaires be completed, and any other evidence (including expert evidence) be provided in accordance with directions given at the first appointment, or any adjournment of that appointment. Without this, as mentioned above, the FDR can be only partially useful (eg as a means of narrowing the issues between the

---

1 Family Proceedings Rules 1991, r 2.74(1)(c) and (f)(ii).
2 *Jenkins v Livesey (formerly Jenkins)* [1985] AC 424, sub nom *Livesey (formerly Jenkins) v Jenkins* [1985] FLR 813, HL; *T v T (Consent Order: Procedure to Set Aside)* [1996] 2 FLR 640, Richard Anelay QC as deputy High Court judge.
3 *Gojkovic v Gojkovic (No 2)* [1992] Fam 40, [1991] 2 FLR 233, CA.
4 And see **3.13** et seq above.

parties); but without full relevant disclosure settlement of the case is impossible[5].

Calderbank correspondence

5.5   Seven days before the appointment (by which is probably meant one week[6]) the applicant is required to file 'all such [*sic*][7] offers and proposals and responses to them'[8] as have passed between the parties. These documents will then be returned to the parties at the end of the FDR and will not be retained in any way on the court file[9].

Parties' attendance at court

5.6   Unless the court orders otherwise, both parties[10] must attend the FDR[11]. Frequently, the FDR date will be fixed when the parties are present in person at the first appointment, or an adjournment thereof. If a client is unavoidably unavailable the court should be told immediately and the district judge asked to give leave for non-attendance of the client or to adjourn[12]; although it is almost inconceivable that an FDR appointment could take place without both parties being present.

Costs estimates

5.7   As with the first appointment and all court hearings, the parties must produce to the district judge an estimate of their solicitor and own client costs incurred to the date of the hearing[13].

---

5 See further **7.9** below.

6 But see true computation of 'seven days' under the Family Proceedings Rules 1991, r 1.5 at **4.2** fn 8 above.

7 It appears that words are missing from the rule as drawn, as a result of it having been taken from a version of the present rule set out in the Draft Rules without the words left out from the Draft Rule having been incorporated into the new sub-rule. The Draft Rule (8(c)) read: 'No offer or proposal made by a party, whether orally or in writing, nor any response to any such offer or proposal, may be excluded from consideration at the appointment by virtue of a claim of privilege'. This remarkable provision has been excluded. The word 'such' in r 2.75(1)(b) refers to the offers and proposals set out in Draft Rule 8(c).

8 Family Proceedings Rules 1991, 2.75(1)(b).

9 Ibid.

10 It should not be overlooked that other parties, such as trustees, might by this time be parties to the proceedings; so 'both parties' must clearly mean the applicant and respondent in this context.

11 Family Proceedings Rules 1991, r 2.75(2).

12 This application, whatever the district judge's decision, seems likely to attract a fee of £20.

13 See full consideration of this question at **4.35** above.

CONDUCT OF THE APPOINTMENT

5.8 In any form of mediation the mediator should take no part in the decision-making: he or she only facilitates decisions. Further, it is public policy that parties be encouraged to negotiate rather than to litigate to a final conclusion; and therefore communications during the course of such negotiations are privileged from discovery[14]. It is axiomatic, therefore, that the district judge who conducts the FDR takes no further part in the proceedings save to conduct any further FDR; and the rules so provide[15].

5.9 The parties are intended to 'use their best endeavours to reach agreement on relevant matters in issue between them'[16]. To assist in this the court may adjourn the FDR. If agreement is reached, a consent order can be made. Failing this the court can give directions including directions for a final hearing. A minatory sub-rule concerning costs is absent here.

---

14 See eg *Rush & Tomkins Ltd v Greater London Council* [1989] AC 1280, [1988] 3 All ER 737, HL; and see **7.2** et seq below.
15 Family Proceedings Rules 1991, r 2.75(1).
16 Ibid, r 2.75(1)(c).

Chapter 6

AFTER THE FINANCIAL DISPUTE RESOLUTION APPOINTMENT

TOWARDS THE HEARING

6.1   If the FDR does not achieve an agreement between the parties, or if the case proceeds direct to a final hearing from the first appointment, the district judge will give directions for the final hearing. These are likely to include directions that:

–   the parties agree a bundle of documents[1] and that these are photocopied, indexed and paginated (normally by the applicant) and lodged at court prior to the hearing[2];
–   the parties prepare, exchange and file at court skeleton arguments prior to the hearing[3];
–   the applicant prepares a chronology (or background summary to the case) and any schedules needed in the particular case, and serves them on the respondent and files them at court prior to the hearing[4];
–   lists of authorities (if any) are exchanged and a bundle of copies of authorities are made available to the court.

6.2   It is beyond the scope of this book to consider preparation for trial in any detail. To a large extent this will depend on the preference of the legal representatives, and especially the advocate in the case (who should, wherever possible, be the same advocate[5] as represented the client at the first appointment and at the FDR (if any)); and listing arrangements may vary a little from court to court. However, two final points need to be made: the first relates to further evidence; and the second relates to the requirement that draft orders sought by a party are required to be submitted to the court.

FURTHER EVIDENCE

6.3   At the first appointment the district judge gives 'directions as to (iii) any evidence sought to be adduced by each party'[6]. It remains to be seen how this provision will be used. The court's powers to refuse to hear relevant

---

1   For a helpful note on preparation of bundles see *B v B (Court Bundles: Video Evidence)* (also known as *Practice Note of 11 November 1993*) [1994] 2 FLR 323, Wall J.
2   Practice will differ from court to court as to how long before the hearing this date will be – probably no more than a day or so.
3   This period might be up to five days or so before the hearing.
4   Ibid.
5   See **4.36** above.
6   Family Proceedings Rules 1991, r 2.74(1)(b)(iii); and see **4.15** above.

evidence are very limited indeed; provided only that, in cases dealt with on affidavit, an affidavit[7] is sworn by the witness whose evidence the party wishes to have available before the court. It would seem prudent to give notice at a directions appointment that such evidence is proposed to be called and to seek from the district judge a direction as to when it is to be filed.

PROPOSED ORDERS

6.4   The Advisory Group on Ancillary Relief was concerned that prior to the hearing the parties should set out their 'final open position' to the court. As it is expressed in the Commentary[8]:

> 'This will force both parties into the open and prevent too much "waiting to see how the evidence emerges"[9] before deciding how or at what level to pitch the case at court.'

Accordingly, the Family Proceedings Rules 1991, r 2.77 orders that each party exchange, one after the other, 'an open statement which sets out concisely the nature and amount of the orders which he[10] proposes to invite the court to make'. First, the applicant must (unless the court otherwise directs) file and serve her statement on the respondent 14 days before the date of the final hearing. 'Not more than 7 [*sic*] days[11] after' such service the respondent reciprocates.

6.5   This is a radical proposal and one so far unknown to family proceedings. It may well be that, in the context of ancillary relief proceedings, this information is privileged from disclosure and that a party cannot therefore be compelled to reveal this, without a change in primary legislation. The further problem remains that facts in family proceedings are not always static[12]. Where the evidence is clearly known and beyond argument then it should be possible to frame the required draft order. But where (to give an easy example) valuation evidence is in dispute, it hardly seems reasonable to expect a figure to be put on a lump sum payment; still less where matters may yet be clarified in cross-examination, or one of the

---

7 In the case of opinion evidence, witness evidence will normally be before the court in the form of a report, and subject to the provisions of Ord 38, r 36: see **4.18** et seq above.

8 Step 15-17 para 2.

9 Quotation marks are as given in the Commentary.

10 Endearingly, this rule makes both applicant and respondent male (as does Family Proceedings Rules 1991, r 2.58) even though, Interpretations Acts notwithstanding, one of them must be female.

11 By this it must be assumed that the rule means a week later (see **4.2** fn 8 above); although this is not what this rule says – if properly interpreted. For if this provision was construed according to the Family Proceedings Rules 1991, r 1.5, service might not occur until almost the day of the hearing (especially if Easter or Christmas intervened).

12 See analysis of this question at **4.4** above.

parties will be found to have failed to disclose[13] details of his financial affairs[14]. To draft an order in such circumstances, before 'the evidence emerges', would seem to invite a claim for professional negligence; and all that then remains between the advocate and his insurers is the unattractive argument of the advocate's immunity[15].

DRAFTING THE ORDER

6.6 The drafting of the order will start from the issues in the case. Onto this will have to be superimposed any undertakings which will be required of one party or the other to give full effect to the order. Finally, any evidential questions[16] still in issue will need to be borne in mind. Practitioners may have their own precedents available to them on disk or hard copy. Failing that, the Solicitors Family Law Association publish a set of precedents[17] which covers the majority of family circumstances. Using a set of precedents such as these provides both an aid to drafting and a useful checklist to ensure that important factors have not been overlooked.

---

13 It is arguable that because of the possibility of failures to disclose that the proposed form of a draft order should remain privileged as between legal adviser and client: a low draft order accepted by a spouse who has failed to give disclosure may lead to injustice which can only be corrected by an application to set aside – and then, only if the non-disclosure later comes to light.

14 Amongst many (no doubt), such expressions as the following spring to mind: per Connell J in *W v W (Periodical Payments: Pensions)* [1996] 2 FLR 480 who was concerned at the 'devious conduct' of the husband who, the judge thought, was not 'genuinely concerned to assist the court to a proper understanding of his financial arrangements'; or Holman J in *F v F (Duxbury Calculation: Rate of Return)* [1996] 1 FLR 833 at 837G of a husband against whom he was to make an indemnity order for costs: he 'has been clearly evasive or less than frank if not actually lying'.

15 Per McKinnon J in *B v Miller & Co* [1996] 2 FLR 23.

16 For a consideration of 'evidential issues', see **4.7** above.

17 Recently commended by Ward LJ in *G v G (Periodical Payments: Jurisdiction)* [1997] 1 FLR 368, CA.

Chapter 7

COSTS AND SETTLEMENT

PROPOSALS TO SETTLE 'WITHOUT PREJUDICE'

7.1 The emphasis in the Scheme upon settlement and the saving of costs will make *Calderbank* correspondence and other attempts to settle all the more important. As has been seen already, the emphasis on concern by the courts to promote settlement has produced the FDR. However, the need to attempt to negotiate goes wider than that: for *Calderbank* correspondence is almost certain to have an important influence on the success of the FDR; and it will influence, although it need not decide, the court in any exercise of its discretion as to costs.

Privilege – negotiations and 'without prejudice' correspondence

7.2 Public policy encourages parties to negotiate to settle their differences rather than litigate them to a finish[1]. Thus, details of all negotiations, whether oral or in writing, are privileged from disclosure in the course of court proceedings[2] or from being given as evidence in court; and any document which is part of the negotiations is privileged from discovery[3]. Similarly, discussions with a view to settlement will be privileged, even though 'without prejudice', or some such words, are not used[4].

Privilege ceases

Waiver

7.3 'Without prejudice' correspondence can be regarded as covered by a form of legal professional privilege. Where a document is covered by such privilege, only the writer – or the client, if it is a letter written by a solicitor on that client's behalf – can waive the privilege; for the confidentiality which resides in the document belongs to the writer or the client alone. Once privilege is waived, then the document may be disclosed. Without such waiver the document (eg a letter written 'without prejudice') remains

---

1 *Cutts v Head* [1984] Ch 290, [1984] 1 All ER 597, CA.
2 Family Proceedings Rules 1991, r 2.75(1)(b) provides a significant exception to this which can only be understood in the context of the district judge who deals with the FDR being excluded thereafter from normal judicial processes.
3 See eg the Rules of the Supreme Court 1965, Ord 24, r 5(2) (considered fully in *The Family Court Practice 1997* (Family Law)); and see eg *Cross & Tapper on Evidence* 8th edn (Butterworths, 1995) pp 500–505.
4 *Chocoladafabriken Lindt v Nestle* [1978] RPC 287.

privileged from disclosure. In the light of this legal principle, the requirement that without prejudice correspondence be filed at court before an
FDR[5] is the more remarkable. Thus, r 2.75(1)(b) of the Family Proceedings
Rules 1991 abolishes a fundamental rule based on long-standing public
policy. It is presumably justified on the basis that the FDR is outside the court
process and that disclosure of the documents is deemed to be essentially
voluntary. For only the client can waive privilege: without any statutory
authority, it is submitted, a rule cannot do so.

Acceptance

7.4   An offer contained in a 'without prejudice' communication can be
accepted. If it is accepted, the communication ceases to be privileged and
can be used in evidence. This will depend, however, on acceptance of the
terms set out in the negotiations in their entirety. Thus, a party cannot
accept certain terms, but not others, and then claim admissibility of the
totality of the without prejudice communications. Ordinary contract
principles apply: for example, to form a contract, an acceptance cannot be
conditional on other counter-proposals being accepted[6]. If an offer is
accepted unconditionally and the privilege is lost, then the correspondence
as a whole is admissible. Whether or not the parties are then held to their
agreement by the courts will depend on normal *Edgar*[7] principles.

Admissions made 'without prejudice'

7.5   An admission or a statement of existing facts or of the strength of a
party's case, even though marked 'without prejudice', is not privileged and
can be treated as admissible evidence at any hearing[8]. Thus, for example,
where a party admits (in the course of negotiations or during an FDR) the
existence of financial information not previously disclosed, evidence as to
that admission can be adduced in subsequent court proceedings; although it
will be for the party alleging the admission to prove it.[9] On this question, a
mediator would be compellable. Whether a district judge on an FDR
appointment would be compellable may be more contentious. As a judge, it
is probable that he is not compellable[10]. However, whether a district judge in
the role of mediator can properly be said to be acting 'in relation to his
judicial functions' is altogether another question. The fact that he is
subsequently precluded from exercising a judicial function in relation to the

---

5 See **5.5** above.

6 The counter-offer has the effect of creating a fresh set of proposals and, in law, the original
   set of proposals are not capable of acceptance: *Hyde v Wrench* (1840) 3 Beav 334.

7 *Edgar v Edgar* (1981) FLR 19, [1981] 1 WLR 1410, CA; and see further **7.12** below.

8 *Buckinghamshire County Council v Moran* [1989] 2 All ER 225, CA.

9 But now see *Practice Direction: Ancillary Relief Procedure: Pilot Scheme (16 June 1997)* [1997] 2
   FLR 304, reproduced at Appendix 3.

10 *Warren v Warren* [1996] 2 FLR 777, CA: 'It is my view that no judge in relation to his judicial
    functions is a compellable witness' – per Lord Woolf MR at 785.

case in hand, and that privilege is removed from documents placed before him, suggests strongly that he cannot be said to be performing a judicial function in any accepted sense of the term. Accordingly, in relation to any admission before him, the district judge may be compellable.

Notice to admit facts

7.6 Before the burden of proving the admission need be considered or the debate on whether or not a district judge is compellable need be engaged, the first step for the party to whom the admission was made should be to give notice to admit the facts of the admission to the party who made it[11]. In the context of the Scheme and its concern for costs, the notice to admit facts is particularly important: if the fact of the admission is admitted, costs will be saved; if it is not admitted, but subsequently proved, the costs of proving the admission will fall in any event on the person who fails to admit[12].

PROPOSALS TO SETTLE: *CALDERBANK* CORRESPONDENCE AND COSTS

Calderbank correspondence

7.7 Not only is it public policy to encourage negotiation; but, especially in the ancillary relief field, parties have been encouraged to set out in correspondence, terms on which they will settle[13]. Where a proposal to settle is marked 'without prejudice' – a *Calderbank*[14] letter – it can also be made subject to the condition[15] that the letter may be referred to the court on the question of costs if, for example, the outcome of an application is to award an applicant less than was offered to her in the *Calderbank* letter. In that case the offeror may be entitled to expect costs to be awarded in his favour from a reasonable time after the date of the *Calderbank* offer.

7.8 The principles derived from *Calderbank* have now been incorporated

---

11 Rules of the Supreme Court 1965, Ord 27, r 2; County Court Rules 1981, Ord 20, r 2, but see *Practice Direction: Ancillary Relief Procedure: Pilot Scheme (16 June 1997)* [1997] 2 FLR 304, reproduced at Appendix 3.

12 Ibid, Ord 62, r 6(7) (r 6(8) if admission of documents is requested).

13 See eg *Gojkovic v Gojkovic (No 2)* [1992] Fam 40, [1991] 2 FLR 233, CA; *A v A (Costs: Appeal)* [1996] 1 FLR 14, Singer J.

14 *Calderbank v Calderbank* [1976] Fam 93, [1975] 3 All ER 333, CA. A *Calderbank* letter is effective only where there has been full disclosure of both parties' means: *Gojkovic v Gojkovic (No 2)* (above).

15 It is conventional to include this condition in a *Calderbank* letter; but strictly it is not necessary. Privilege can always be waived by the person to whom it belongs (see **7.3** above). Thus at the end of a hearing, when costs fall to be decided, privilege can be waived and any offer put forward by a party can be referred to the court.

into the rules[16] so that the importance of 'without prejudice' correspondence in this context is emphasised. However, a *Calderbank* letter may not be referred to the court, according to the rules[17], 'until the question of costs falls to be decided'[18]; save that under the Scheme it is a prerequisite of the FDR that 'offers and proposals and responses to them' be put to the court[19].

Prerequisites of a *Calderbank* offer

7.9   In ancillary relief proceedings the effectiveness of a *Calderbank* offer depends on the following:

(1)   *Full relevant disclosure* – a *Calderbank* offer can be effective only once there has been full relevant disclosure[20]; for without such disclosure the other party cannot reasonably be expected to respond.

(2)   *Response to the offer* – once disclosure is complete, then it is incumbent upon the recipient of the offer to respond within a reasonable time[21]. If there is no response, a party risks no award of costs even though an offer is beaten[22].

(3)   *Offer in time* – if an offer is made late, a party may not be entitled to his costs[23].

Calderbank correspondence and legal aid

7.10   Where the applicant has legal aid, her legal representative must ensure that, if a *Calderbank* offer is not accepted, consideration is given to referring the matter to the Legal Aid Board; for all 'reasonable offers of settlement' must be brought to the attention of the Board[24]. If the respondent is unassisted, he should ensure that the Board is aware of any *Calderbank* offer . If he does not do so, he risks failing on application for costs under the Legal Aid Act 1988 s 18[25].

---

16 See eg Rules of the Supreme Court 1965, Ord 22, r 14 (*Calderbank* letters); Ord 62, r 9 (effect of *Calderbank* correspondence on awards of costs).

17 This is the position provided for by the rules. However, applying the normal rules of waiver of privilege at the instance of the person to whom the confidentiality belongs (see **7.3** above), it would seem unnecessary to reserve the right to refer the letter to the court on costs since it is open to the party concerned at any time in the proceedings to waive privilege and to make their own *Calderbank* correspondence available to the court.

18 Rules of the Supreme Court 1965, Ord 22, r 14; County Court Rules 1981, Ord 11, r 10.

19 Family Proceedings Rules 1991, r 2.75(1)(b); and see **5.5** above.

20 *Gojkovic v Gojkovic (No 2)* [1992] Fam 40, [1991] 2 FLR 233, CA per Butler-Sloss LJ.

21 *A v A (Costs: Appeal)* [1996] 1 FLR 14, Singer J. In that case the learned judge suggested three weeks as the appropriate period.

22 *S v S (Financial Provision)* [1990] 2 FLR 252, CA.

23 *Gojkovic v Gojkovic (No 2)* [1992] Fam 40, [1991] 2 FLR 233, CA.

24 Civil Legal Aid (General) Regulations 1989, reg 70(1)(b).

25 And see *Re Spurling's Will Trusts, Philpot v Philpot* [1966] 1 All ER 745, [1966] 1 WLR 920 considered fully in *The Family Court Practice 1997* (Family Law) under the Legal Aid Act 1988, s 18.

Moderation and the *Calderbank* offer

7.11 Finally, it is essential that any proposal by an applicant to settle, or a response to a *Calderbank* offer, be pitched at a level which is reasonable. If not, even if the applicant beats the offer, she risks losing part or all of her costs[26].

AGREEMENT ON PROPOSALS TO SETTLE

Agreements – *Edgar* principles

7.12 Spouses may not, by their own agreement, preclude the courts from exercising jurisdiction over their financial arrangements[27]. Parties should expect the courts to 'start from the position that a solemn and freely negotiated bargain ... ought to be adhered to unless some clear and compelling reason ... is shown to the contrary'[28] (eg a drastic change of circumstances). Thus an agreement cannot bind the court; but in considering what weight should be given to it the courts will generally have regard to the classic dictum of Ormrod LJ:

> 'It is not necessary in this connection to think in formal legal terms, such as misrepresentation or estoppel, *all* the circumstances as they affect two human beings must be considered in the complex relationship of marriage. So, the circumstances surrounding the making of the agreement are relevant. Undue pressure by one side, exploitation of a dominant position to secure an unreasonable advantage, inadequate knowledge, possibly bad legal advice, an important change of circumstances, unforeseen or overlooked at the time of making the agreement, are all relevant to the issue of justice between the parties.'[29]

7.13 Thus, so far as agreements between spouses are concerned, provided they are 'properly and fairly arrived at with competent legal advice [they] should not be displaced unless there are good and substantial grounds for concluding that an injustice will be done by holding the parties'[30] to their terms. Exceptions to this proposition will be rare. An example of such an exception might be fairness in the eye of the 'independent bystander'[31];

---

26 See eg *Phillips v Peace* [1996] 2 FLR 230, [1996] 2 FCR 237, Johnson J (applicant lost part of her costs because her claim was pitched too high).

27 Matrimonial Causes Act 1973, s 34(1); *Hyman v Hyman* [1929] AC 601, HL.

28 *Edgar v Edgar* (1981) FLR 19, [1981] 1 WLR 1410, CA per Oliver LJ at FLR 31H.

29 Ibid, at FLR 25C.

30 Ibid, per Ormrod LJ at FLR 25F.

31 '... if any independent bystander had been asked to consider the arrangement that was being put forward in 1975, he would have been bound to say that it was an unfair arrangement so far as the wife was concerned': *Camm v Camm* (1983) FLR 577, CA per Sir Roger Ormrod at 585D.

although it is only likely that extreme unfairness or a radical change of circumstances will alter the general proposition in *Edgar*[32].

Agreement leading to a court order

7.14   Where the agreement leads to a consent order – whether after an FDR or following negotiations between parties in mediation or with their solicitors – then, provided that both parties had legal advice, the test for setting aside the court order, even on the basis of manifestly bad legal advice, is considerably more stringent than the *Edgar* test[33] – where there has, as yet, been no order.

Consent order and bad legal advice

7.15   In *Harris v Manahan*, the court took the view that the wife applicant had plainly had bad legal advice – she had been advised to settle on terms that ignored her need for continuing financial support from her husband and to turn down an advantageous sale of the former matrimonial home. However, bad legal advice was a factor which, said Ward LJ, the court could take into account only in the most exceptional of circumstances. Generally, it was more important that there be finality in litigation. 'Only in the most exceptional case of the cruellest injustice will the public interest in the finality of litigation be put aside'[34]; and, said Ward LJ, *Harris* was not such a case. Ward LJ agreed with Connell J (the judge at first instance) in his distinguishing of the approach of the court as between agreements and consent orders: 'it would not be right to add bad legal advice to the list of considerations which can justify the setting aside of consent orders'[35]. Ward LJ differs only in that he would still allow in the case of 'the cruellest injustice'; and he specifically holds that, in such a consideration, whether or not the wife will be able successfully to claim against her solicitors should be ignored[36].

---

32 Rare recent examples of agreements overturned include *Beach v Beach* [1995] 2 FLR 160, Thorpe J and *B v B (Consent Order: Variation)* [1995] 1 FLR 9, Thorpe J. To every reported instance of an agreement overturned there are probably five or more reported examples of agreements upheld including *Pounds v Pounds* [1994] 1 FLR 775, [1994] 1 WLR 1535, CA; *Smith v McInerney* [1994] 2 FLR 1077, Thorpe J; *Hewitson v Hewitson* [1995] 1 FLR 241, [1995] 2 WLR 287, CA; *Benson v Benson (Deceased)* [1996] 1 FLR 692, Bracewell J.
33 *Harris v Manahan* [1997] 1 FLR 205, CA.
34 Ibid, at 225E.
35 Ibid, at 223B.
36 Ibid, at 223E; and see *B v Miller & Co* [1996] 2 FLR 23, McKinnon J (QBD).

Chapter 8

OPERATION OF THE SCHEME: OTHER FORMS OF FINANCIAL RELIEF

INTRODUCTION

8.1   As can be seen from the Commentary, the Scheme is designed very much with the standard ancillary relief application in mind, with other forms of ancillary relief – which are undoubtedly covered by the Scheme – left to make their way as best they may through the courts. What follows can only be one practitioner's opinion as to what may be done in a court to which the Scheme applies. It makes no claim to be any more authoritative than that.

8.2   In the consideration of these applications the following skeleton of the process under the Scheme will be assumed:

(1)   *Applications in Form A or B* – applications are commenced[1] on Form A (ancillary relief) or Form B (applications under the Matrimonial Causes Act 1973, s 10(2) which, for the purposes of this procedure, has been added to the list of proceedings for ancillary relief).

(2)   *Form E – sworn statement of means* – seven weeks before the First Appointment both parties file, and serve on each other, Form E (statement of means and of their case)[2].

(3)   *First Appointment* – the objective of the first appointment[3] is to define the issues and the saving of costs and at that appointment the district judge gives directions including referral of the application for a Financial Dispute Resolution ('FDR').

(4)   *Financial Dispute Resolution* – the FDR appointment[4] is 'a meeting held for the purposes of conciliation' at which the district judge may try to assist the parties to reach agreement. That district judge then has no further involvement in the case, save for any other FDR.

(5)   *Hearing* – if no agreement is reached at the FDR the district judge can give directions for the final hearing[5]; and the parties proceed accordingly. Before the hearing the parties must, sequentially, file details of the order they seek from the court[6].

(6)   *Costs* – the Scheme expresses its concern over costs by requiring that, at every hearing, each party shall produce a written estimate of costs[7].

---

1 Family Proceedings Rules 1991, r 2.72; and see Ch 2.
2 Ibid, r 2.73; and see Ch 3.
3 Ibid, r 2.74(1); and see Ch 4.
4 Ibid, r 2.75; and see Ch 5.
5 Ibid, rr 2.74(1)(d)(iii) and 2.75(1)(d).
6 Ibid, r 2.77; and see Ch 6.
7 Ibid, r 2.76; and see Ch 7, and **4.10** and **5.7** above.

INTERIM ORDERS

8.3 The term 'interim orders' in this context is intended to imply the following:

– interim orders for periodical payments (for payment of maintenance pending suit);
– interim lump sums under the Matrimonial Causes Act 1973, s 23 (insofar as these may be available[8]).

8.4 The Family Proceedings Rules 1991, r 2.74(1)(d)(ii) and (f)(i) refer specifically to the question of interim periodical payments; but by this time at least 10 weeks, and probably longer, will have passed since issue of the application. It may well be that the applicant will require interim periodical payments (or maintenance pending suit) or an interim lump sum to cover expenses, including to cover mortgage repayments, solicitor's costs and so on as a matter of urgency. Therefore, there seems to be no reason why application should not be added to the wording of Form A or Form B[9], accompanied by a traditional affidavit, along the lines of the following:

'AND FURTHER TAKE NOTICE THAT the [petitioner/respondent] intends to apply to the district judge at [name of court venue] on   day the   day of   199   at   o'clock for an order for interim maintenance pending suit and, thereafter, periodical payments and for an interim lump sum to cover expenses; and the grounds on which this application is made are set out in the [petitioner's/respondent's] affidavit filed herewith.

Time estimate: . [Continue as in Form A or B].

This course need not in any way impede the Form E and first appointment procedure. Form E will still need to be filed and the first appointment can go ahead in the usual way. Indeed, the interim order could be made interim until the first appointment. The affidavit in support will deal with such matters as:

– why the applicant needs the order as a matter of urgency and on an interim basis;

---

8 This is not the place to debate whether or not interim lump sums may be available to cover expenses such as a wife's anticipated legal fees (*per contra* see *Sears Tooth (A Firm) v Payne Hicks Beach (A Firm) and Others* [1997] 2 FLR 116, Wilson J and the statutory charge in respect of the solicitor's lien under the Solicitors Act 1974, s 73).

9 If the standard Form A/B is used this addition will not fit well; but in such circumstances the wording alone should be used above the precedent suggested here. If two forms of application are made (Form A and the interim application) then two fees will be charged.

- her own income position, and that of the children[10];
- her needs in terms of payments from income: ie a breakdown of her weekly or monthly expenditure;
- her needs for a lump sum payment, eg for payment of mortgage arrears, a deposit on a flat to which she will be forced to move from the former matrimonial home, solicitor's fees; and note that a lump sum can be paid by instalments.

VARIATION OF PERIODICAL PAYMENTS

8.5 The Scheme covers applications for variation and discharge of periodical payments[11]. There is little to be said about the procedure for this; in principle an application for periodical payments can proceed under the Scheme. It must be questioned, however, whether it can be said that an application for variation of periodical payments pursued under the Scheme could ever remotely save costs relative to an application under existing procedures. Were it possible to produce an abbreviated Form E and to make the first appointment a final hearing then the costs position might not be greatly altered by the Scheme.

CHILDREN APPLICATIONS

8.6 Applications for periodical payments for children will be rare[12]; but where they can be made they are plainly included in the term 'ancillary relief'[13]. If made with application for other relief by an applicant parent they will be covered by the Scheme in conventional form. However, an application for periodical payments can also be made for a child of the family in Matrimonial Causes Act 1973 proceedings but otherwise on a free-standing basis[14]: that is to say, not alongside any other application for

---

10 In view of the fact that no interim child support maintenance is available under the Child Support Act 1991, and of the delays of the Child Support Agency in assessing such maintenance, if no money is being paid to the applicant at all and she has independent children, interim payments for herself will be her only means of obtaining support for the family; but suitable undertakings concerning any payment of child support maintenance will then be needed.

11 See definition of ancillary relief in the Family Proceedings Rules 1991, r 1.2(1) and **2.2** above.

12 Child Support Act 1991, s 8(3); but see s 8(5)–(8) and applications for non-qualifying children (Child Support Act 1991, s 44).

13 Ie all forms of application for financial provision, which includes child periodical payments, are covered by the definition of ancillary relief: Matrimonial Causes Act 1973, s 21(1)(b) and Family Proceedings Rules 1991, r 1.2(1).

14 Family Proceedings Rules 1991, r 2.54(1) which lists the people who may make such an application including anyone in whose favour a residence order is made, a local authority, the Official Solicitor where appointed as guardian ad litem, and the child (with leave).

ancillary relief by a parent. Any such application is capable, in theory, of being dealt with under the Scheme, as indeed it must be; but Form E seems hardly appropriate to, for example, grandparents who might have a residence order, still less to the local authority or the Official Solicitor[15].

Child with leave

8.7   For a child over 19[16] whose parents have been involved in Matrimonial Causes Act 1973 proceedings, and who seeks periodical payments (eg to make up his or her grant) the ancillary relief route is the only means of application to the court for that child. Some of the requirements of Form E (eg date of separation of the parties, questions of conduct and contribution) seem scarcely appropriate for completion by a child; but as drafted the rules make Form E obligatory[17]: it is not even open to the district judge, on directions being sought, to dispense with it for a 'child' in these circumstances.

AVOIDANCE OF DISPOSITION ORDERS

8.8   An application for an avoidance of disposition order[18] is ancillary relief for the purposes of the Scheme[19]. Procedure for the obtaining of such an order is set out in *The Family Court Practice 1997* (Family Law)[20]. If the need for the order is known at the time of the application in Form A or Form B, application for the avoidance of disposition order can be included in form at that stage; otherwise it can be made as a separate application after Form A or B has been filed.

8.9   In theory, the Form E/first appointment procedure can then be followed. Indeed, Form E provides a box[21] for indication that an avoidance of disposition order is sought. However, given the urgency which such applications often need to be dealt with and the fact that extensive information may be necessary for the court to make the order, the following steps should, in addition, be taken:

–   A separate affidavit should be filed containing all the additional information needed for proof of the application.

---

15 It is accepted that any such application as this will be rare (for example, in respect of a qualifying child, anyone with a residence order as a person with care will have to apply under the Child Support Act 1991) but such applications are possible; and to avoid any difficulty they could have been exempted from the Scheme.

16 Ie no longer covered by the Child Support Act 1991.

17 Family Proceedings Rules 1991, r 2.73(1).

18 Matrimonial Causes Act 1973, s 37(2)(b).

19 Family Proceedings Rules 1991, rr 1.2(1) and 2.71(1).

20 Procedural Guide No 22.

21 Part 5(d).

–   Leave should be sought from the court for the filing with that affidavit of further documentation (if any) to avoid any criticism by the court in view of the general embargo on the filing of documents after the filing of an application in Form A[22]. The request for such leave should be included in the affidavit in support of the application.

–   Directions should be sought as soon as possible as to the conduct of the application, to include the question of the disponee being joined as a party to the proceedings[23]; and as to whether an FDR appointment is appropriate if the disponee is joined. If practicable, the application for avoidance of disposition should be heard at the same time as the application for ancillary relief[24].

VARIATION OF SETTLEMENT

8.10   An application for variation of settlement can be made in the usual way in Form A and pursued by means of the Form E/first appointment procedure. The trustees will need to be served[25]. At the first appointment the court will then need to consider whether any children affected by the application need to be separately represented[26]; if so, who should be their guardian ad litem; and, presumably, what sort of involvement (if any) they should have at the FDR.

---

22 Family Proceedings Rules 1991, r 2.73(3).
23 *Tebbutt v Haynes* [1981] 2 All ER 238.
24 Family Proceedings Rules 1991, r 2.62(2).
25 Ibid, r 2.59(3)(a); and see **3.8** above.
26 Ibid, r 2.57.

Chapter 9

POSTSCRIPT

ADVERSARIAL AND INQUISITORIAL

9.1 Seen alongside the Woolf Report[1], the Scheme suggests a debate on the inquisitorial as against the adversarial system of justice. Before the relative merits of these two systems can be debated the question of the justice which a family court system seeks to achieve should be considered; how it is to be achieved and at what cost to the litigant?

9.2 In a case where facts are in issue, justice is concerned with seeking to achieve a clear assessment of the truth. Where points of law are at issue the court will be concerned to establish a correct interpretation of the law as applied to the facts of the case. Where the regulation of rights is in issue (as with residence of children, disposition of matrimonial property or judicial review) the court will be concerned to achieve fairness[2]. To achieve fairness, it will normally be necessary to attempt a correct interpretation of the law (where a point of law is involved); but it will not always be necessary to arrive at a clear assessment of the truth.

Attaining justice and fairness

9.3 The common law has developed the adversarial system to arrive at an assessment of truth and thereby to achieve justice. By this means, a proposition is advanced by one party and contradicted by an opposing party. Parties to the debate are entitled to call their own evidence and to challenge the evidence of other parties. The culmination of the debate is the trial at which oral evidence is given and challenged before a referee, the judge, who then (in almost all civil proceedings) determines the outcome of the debate by giving judgment as between the parties. In the classic model of the system, the judge will have had no contact with the case until the trial; although increasingly nowadays the judge who is to hear the case gives directions prior to the final hearing.

9.4 By contrast, many legal systems based on Roman Law and/or the Code Napoleon, have derived an inquisitorial system where it is the judge's responsibility to seek the truth, once process has been commenced. Thus the instructions judge will largely control what evidence is available to the court and what questions are asked of any witnesses. The final hearing (by

---

1 *Access to Justice: Final Report* by Lord Woolf MR, (HMSO, July 1996).
2 'Fairness' – that is to say equity based on the court's discretion or, in terms of the origin of equity, the 'conscience' of the court.

which time the court's reception of evidence will be closed) will be based on brief argument from the papers (rather than on oral evidence) before the court.

Discretionary jurisdiction

9.5   Procedure in family courts has been adapted, primarily, from procedure in the existing civil courts jurisdiction. This is designed, principally, to test truth and establish points of law. By contrast, the family jurisdiction is concerned mostly to establish rights and responsibility in terms of the welfare of children and of distribution of matrimonial or family property. With important exceptions, matters of law (as distinct from points of procedure, evidence or jurisdiction) and of statutory construction are rarely involved. Moreover, the family lawyer, as advocate, is concerned with an argument over the way in which the court should exercise its discretion in relation to a particular set of family circumstances, rather than dealing with statutory construction or establishment of liability from a given set of facts.

9.6   That the family court process has derived from civil procedures means that its development has largely overlooked the extent to which the court's jurisdiction is based upon exercise of judicial discretion[3]. Statute has imposed upon judges a duty to act in an interventionist way[4], for which the system does not properly allow. The Scheme is an example of an attempt to redress this and to seek for the district judge a more interventionist role.

9.7   Lord Woolf's proposals involve a large measure of inquisitorial process being grafted onto the preparatory stages of the adversarial process. To what extent this will have repercussions for the family lawyer; and to what extent – with an eye also to Lord Woolf's report – family court procedures should adapt to recognise the inquisitorial processes already inherent in them are dealt with below.

---

3   In the context of discretion, it may be instructive to compare our system with that in, for example, France. There the judge exercises his or her discretion in reordering the parties' affairs following divorce; but on a minimum of information and (by English standards) only a cursory court hearing. Property adjustment, where it is possible, is dealt with in a civil, not a family court, in separate and subsequent proceedings.

4   See eg Matrimonial Causes Act 1973, s 1(3): 'On presentation of a petition it shall be the duty of the court to enquire ...'; MCA 1973, s 25(1): 'It shall be the duty of the court *in deciding whether* ...' (ie the court has an option, regardless of the representations of the parties; the words in italics are also used in the Inheritance (Provision for Family and Dependants) Act 1975, s 3(1)); MCA 1973, s 25(2) and the Children Act 1989, s 1(3): '... the court shall in particular have regard to ...'; MCA 1973 s 25A(1): '... it shall be the duty of the court to consider whether it would be appropriate so to exercise [its] powers ...'; Family Proceedings Rules 1991, r 2.62(4): 'At the hearing of an application for ancillary relief the district judge shall ... investigate the allegations, ... and may at any stage of the proceedings ... order the attendance of any person [or the discovery of documents]'.

To what extent inquisitorial?

9.8   In answering the question of the extent to which inquisitorial processes should be adapted into the family proceedings, it is necessary to ask what, in each type of case, the court is seeking to achieve:

(1)   an assessment of the truth of allegations;
(2)   a definition of a point of law or statutory construction; or
(3)   a fair exercise of a discretion vested in the court.

9.9   The vast majority of family cases will come within the last category; but it is necessary briefly to examine each:

(1) Assessment of truth

Where disposal of the case turns on the question of the truthfulness of a witness or the comparison of two or more versions of events, then this is pre-eminently the preserve of the adversarial process involving, if possible, live evidence and cross-examination of witnesses.

(2) Points of law

Adjudication on questions of law or statutory construction are, again, essentially the preserve of a debate on the questions at issue, but between lawyers and involving no oral evidence.

(3) Exercise of discretion

Where the court is required to exercise its discretion in relation to a set of facts, then properly to do so the judge must be prepared to enter the arena, not least so that he or she can tell the parties what aspects of the case the court wishes to consider to enable it to exercise its discretion. Here is the area where an element of the inquisitorial process must impinge upon the pre-existing adversarial procedures.

9.10   If it is accepted that the vast majority of cases in the family jurisdiction involve entirely – or to a substantial extent – an exercise of the court's discretion, then it is necessary to look at how inquisitorial processes can fairly be introduced into the present, essentially adversarial, process. In doing so, law reformers need to be clear on the distinction between the court's function as referee of an adversarial process (the judge) and its role as director of the process as part of its inquisitorial function.

Case management

9.11   The process of disposing of a case can be divided into:

(a)   the administration of the procedure from issue of an application to its trial or other disposal ('case management'); and
(b)   the adjudication of the issues raised by the application.

9.12   The need for case management has already been identified by the judiciary[5]. This then throws up a tension between the judiciary and the courts administration on the one hand and the parties and their advisers on the other. This is the central question for Woolf. In the family proceedings context, this resolves itself into the following main areas:

(1)   timetabling;
(2)   dispute resolution – mediation either in court or by adjournment for outside mediation;
(3)   definition of the issues;
(4)   oversight of nature and extent of evidence, including discovery;
(5)   oversight of expert evidence, including reports from the Official Solicitor, court welfare officers and guardians ad litem;
(6)   control of the trial.

The Scheme deals with (1)–(5) on this list; and if these are dealt with satisfactorily, it could be said that, in terms of case management, everything possible has been done in preparation for (6). Control is then a matter for the judge on the day.

PROPOSALS AND AMENDMENTS

Points of principle

9.13   Points of principle which still need debate include the following:

Rules of evidence
To what extent should the rules of evidence as to, for example, discovery, legal professional privilege and control by the court of the relevant evidence to be called, be altered; and if they are to be altered, does this need primary legislation?

Court control of procedure
To what extent is it preferable that the court assumes direct control of certain aspects of the process: for example, serving documents, such as the application, on the parties; and penalising on its own initiative delays in the filing of documents (especially Form E, or its equivalent).

Points of detail

9.14   Points of detail in the present version of the Scheme need to be ironed out, including the following:

---

5 See eg *Practice Direction of 31 January 1995 (Case Management)* [1995] 1 FLR 456, [1995] 1 WLR 332; Children Act Advisory Committee annual reports.

(a)   the lack of any reference to Form E in the existing rules, which continue to apply to the Scheme;

(b)   the lacuna and inconsistencies which exist for most ancillary relief applications which do not conform to the standard financial provision and property adjustment order application process (eg variation of settlement, children applications, variations of periodical payments, applications where there is a mortgage on the former matrimonial home and so on);

(c)   the failure to note what 'seven days' means under Family Proceedings Rules 1991, r 1.5;

(d)   the words omitted from the Family Proceedings Rules 1991, r 2.75(1)(b).

Appendix 1

PROCEDURAL GUIDE

All references in column 3 are to the Family Proceedings Rules 1991 (as amended), unless otherwise stated.

Applicant	Either spouse: described here as 'applicant' and 'respondent'	rr 2.53(1) and 2.58(1) r 2.72(4)(b)
Which court?	Where the court is listed as part of the Scheme, then: the court in which a matrimonial cause commenced by one or other spouse in proceeding: **Note:** if cause is transferred to a court outside the Scheme the application proceeds as if steps taken as if Scheme not in effect	r 2.71(2) r 2.71(1) r 2.71(5)
Application	Application in Form A **Fee:** £50 £120	r 2.72(2)
Service	By applicant upon: (1) the respondent (2) any mortgagee (3) trustees and settlor of settlement sought to be varied (4) disponee: avoidance of disposition order application	r 2.72(4)(b) r 2.59(4) r 2.59(3)(a) r 2.59(3)(b)
Time for service (by reference to above)	(1) 'within 4 days ... of the filing of the application' (2) ⎫ (3) ⎬ not clear and see **3.6** above (4) ⎭	r 2.72(4)(b) (contrast r 2.72 (4)(b) with r 2.59(3) and (4) re trustees/ mortgagees and affidavit in support of application (Form E))

Notice of first appointment	Notice: in Form C – served with Form A as at 4 and 5	r 2.72(4)(b)
	Date: 10–14 weeks from filing of Form A	r 2.72(4)(a)
Information as to means of parties	**Note:** no discovery can 'be sought or given' after filing of form	r 2.73(3)
	Form E prepared by parties	r 2.73(2)
	Form E exchanged 'simultaneously' by parties	r 2.73(1)
Before first appointment (see below)	(1) Parties file and exchange (a) questionnaire seeking further information	r 2.73(4)(a)
	(b) list of further documents sought	r 2.73(4)(b)
	(c) list of issues	r 2.73(4)(c)
	(d) confirmation of service on pension trustees	r 2.73(4)(d)
	Date: '7 days' before hearing (2) Estimate of costs	r 2.76
	Date: produce at court hearing	
First appointment	Directions given as to (1) Answers to questionnaire	r 2.74(1)(a)(i)
	(2) Documents to be produced	r 2.74(1)(a)(ii)
	(3) Valuation of assets and other expert evidence (and meeting of experts)	r 2.74(1)(b)(i) and (ii); RSC Ord 38, r 38
	(4) Chronologies etc	r 2.74(1)(b)(iii)
	(5) Interim orders	r 2.74(1)(d)(ii) and (f)(i)
	(6) Adjourn for FDR	r 2.74(1)(c)
	Consideration of costs: obligatory	r 2.74(1)(e)
	Note: personal attendance of clients	r 2.74(4)
Before FDR	(1) Applicant files all 'without prejudice' correspondence	
	Date: 7 days before appointment	r 2.75(1)(b)
	(2) Estimate of costs	
	Date: produce at court hearing	r 2.76

Financial Dispute Resolution appointment ('FDR')	Both parties attend	r 2.75(2)
	(1) Court makes consent order;	r 2.75(1)(d)
	(2) Adjourns for further FDR; or	r 2.75(1)(d)
	(3) Gives directions for final hearing and fixes date	r 2.75(1)(d)
	Note: district judge who conducts FDR takes no further part in proceedings	r 2.75(1)(a)
Before final hearing	Open statement as to the order sought by applicant	r 2.77(1)
	Date: not less than 14 days before hearing	
	Open statement as to the order sought by respondent	r 2.77(2)
	Date: not more than '7 days' after service of applicant's statement	

Appendix 2

FAMILY PROCEEDINGS RULES 1991 (SI 1991/ 1247), RR 2.45 AND 2.52–2.77 (AS AMENDED BY THE FAMILY PROCEEDINGS (AMENDMENT) (NO 2) RULES 1997 (SI 1997/1056)

This appendix reproduces the Family Proceedings Rules 1991, rr 2.45 and 2.52 to 2.77 as they apply to proceedings subject to the ancillary relief pilot scheme. Where a rule differs from that otherwise applicable, a supplemental note explains the difference.

2.45 Application under section 10(2) of Act of 1973

(1) An application by a respondent to a petition for divorce for the court to consider the financial position of the respondent after the divorce shall be made by notice in Form B.

...

(4) The powers of the court on hearing the application may be exercised by the district judge.

(5) Where the petitioner has relied on the fact of two or five years' separation and the court has granted a decree nisi without making any finding as to any other fact mentioned in section 1(2) of the Act of 1973, the proper officer shall fix an appointment for the hearing; and rules 2.62(3) to (7) and 10.10 shall apply as if the application were an application for ancillary relief.

(6) A statement of any of the matters mentioned in section 10(3) of the Act of 1973 with respect to which the court is satisfied, or, where the court has proceeded under section 10(4), a statement that the conditions for which that subsection provides have been fulfilled, shall be entered in the records of the court.

Note: In courts covered by the pilot scheme, r 2.45(2), (3) does not apply: see r 2.71(3)(a). In courts covered by the pilot scheme, references to Form M12 are to be construed as references to Form B in Appendix 1A to the rules (not reproduced): see r 2.71(3)(f).

Ancillary relief

2.52 Right to be heard on ancillary questions

A respondent may be heard on any question of ancillary relief without filing an answer and whether or not he has returned to the court office an acknowledgement of service stating his wish to be heard on that question.

2.53 Application by petitioner or respondent for ancillary relief
(1) Any application by a petitioner, or by a respondent who files an answer claiming relief, for—

    (a)   an order for maintenance pending suit,
    (b)   a financial provision order,
    (c)   a property adjustment order,

shall be made in the petition or answer, as the case may be.

(2) Notwithstanding anything in paragraph (1), an application for ancillary relief which should have been made in the petition or answer may be made subsequently—

    (a)   by leave of the court, either by notice in Form A or at the trial, or
    (b)   where the parties are agreed upon the terms of the proposed order, without leave by notice in Form A.

(3) An application by a petitioner or respondent for ancillary relief, not being an application which is required to be made in the petition or answer, shall be made by notice in Form A.

Note: in courts covered by the pilot scheme, references to Form M11 are to be construed as references to Form A in Appendix 1A to the rules (not reproduced): see r 2.71(3)(f).

2.54 Application by parent, guardian etc for ancillary relief in respect of children
(1) Any of the following persons, namely—

    (a)   a parent or guardian of any child of the family,
    (b)   any person in whose favour a residence order has been made with respect to a child of the family, and any applicant for such an order,
    (c)   any other person who is entitled to apply for a residence order with respect to a child,
    (d)   a local authority, where an order has been made under section 30(1)(a) of the Act of 1989 placing a child in its care,
    (e)   the Official Solicitor, if appointed the guardian ad litem of a child of the family under rule 9.5, and
    (f)   a child of the family who has been given leave to intervene in the cause for the purpose of applying for ancillary relief,

may apply for an order for ancillary relief as respects that child by notice in Form A.

(2) In this rule 'residence order' has the meaning assigned to it by section 8(1) of the Act of 1989.

Note: in courts covered by the pilot scheme, references to Form M11 are to be construed as references to Form A in Appendix 1A to the rules (not reproduced): see r 2.71(3)(f).

2.55 Application in Form A or B
Where an application for ancillary relief is made by notice in Form A or an application under rule 2.45 is made by notice in Form B the notice shall be filed—

(a)   if the case is pending in a divorce county court, in that court, or

(b)   if the case is pending in the High Court, in the registry in which it is proceeding ...

Note: in courts covered by the pilot scheme, r 2.55 is redundant, since issue and court for issue are dealt with respectively by rr 2.72(4) and 2.71(1).

2.56 Application for ancillary relief after order of magistrates' court

Where an application for ancillary relief is made while there is in force an order of a magistrates' court for maintenance of a spouse or child, the applicant shall file a copy of the order on or before the hearing of the application.

2.57 Children to be separately represented on certain applications

(1) Where an application is made to the High Court or a divorce county court for an order for a variation of settlement, the court shall, unless it is satisfied that the proposed variation does not adversely affect the rights or interests of any children concerned, direct that the children be separately represented on the application, either by a solicitor or by a solicitor and counsel, and may appoint the Official Solicitor or other fit person to be guardian ad litem of the children for the purpose of the application.

(2) On any other application for ancillary relief the court may give such a direction or make such appointment as it is empowered to give or make by paragraph (1).

(3) Before a person other than the Official Solicitor is appointed guardian ad litem under this rule there shall be filed a certificate by the solicitor acting for the children that the person proposed as guardian has no interest in the matter adverse to that of the children and that he is a proper person to be such guardian.

2.58 General provisions as to evidence etc on application for ancillary relief

(1) A petitioner or respondent who has applied for ancillary relief in his petition or answer and who intends to proceed with the application before a district judge shall, subject to rule 2.67, file a notice in Form A and within four days after doing so serve a copy on the other spouse.

Note: in courts covered by the pilot scheme, r 2.58 is redundant, since issue and service are dealt with by r 2.72(4).

2.59 Evidence on application for property adjustment or avoidance of disposition order

...

(2) Where an application for a property adjustment order or an avoidance of disposition order relates to land, the notice in Form A shall identify the land and—

(a)   state whether the title to the land is registered or unregistered and, if registered, the Land Registry title number; and

(b)   give particulars, so far as known to the applicant, of any mortgage of the land or any interest therein.

(3) A copy of Form A as the case may be, together with a copy of the supporting affidavit, shall be served on the following persons as well as on the respondent to the application, that is to say—

(a)   in the case of an application for an order for a variation of settlement, the trustees of the settlement and the settlor if living;

(b)   in the case of an application for an avoidance of disposition order, the person in whose favour the disposition is alleged to have been made;

and such other persons, if any, as the district judge may direct.

(4) In the case of an application to which paragraph (2) refers, a copy of Form A as the case may be, shall be served on any mortgagee of whom particulars are given pursuant to that paragraph; any person so served may apply to the court in writing, within 14 days after service, for a copy of the applicant's affidavit.

(5) Any person who—

(a)   is served with an affidavit pursuant to paragraph (3), or

(b)   receives an affidavit following an application made in accordance with paragraph (4),

may, within 14 days after service or receipt, as the case may be, file an affidavit in answer.

Note: in courts covered by the pilot scheme, r 2.59(1) does not apply: see r 2.71(3)(a); references to Forms M11 and M13 are to be construed as references to Form A in Appendix 1A to the rules (not reproduced): see r 2.71(3)(f). Further, this rule should presumably be read as if, for references to 'affidavit' in r 2.59(3), (4), (5)(a), (b), a reference to 'Form E' is substituted. Other procedural problems remain in connection with some applications covered by this rule: see **8.8** above.

2.60 Service of affidavit in answer or reply

(1) ... Where the affidavit contains an allegation of adultery or of an improper association with a named person, then, if the court so directs, it shall be endorsed with a notice in Form F and a copy of the affidavit or of such part thereof as the court may direct, indorsed as aforesaid, shall be served on that person by the person who files the affidavit, and the person against whom the allegation is made shall be entitled to intervene in the proceedings by applying for directions under rule 2.74(3) within eight days of service of the notice on him.

(2) Rule 2.37(3) shall apply to a person served with an affidavit under paragraph (1) of this rule as it applies to a co-respondent.

Note: in courts covered by the pilot scheme, r 2.60(1) applies in an amended form: see r 2.71(3)(d), (e); references to Form M14 are to be construed as references to Form F in Appendix 1A to the rules (not reproduced): see r 2.71(3)(f). Further, this rule should presumably be read as if, for all references to 'affidavit', 'Form E' is substituted.

2.61 Information on application for consent order for financial relief
(1) Subject to paragraphs (2) and (3), there shall be lodged with every application for a consent order under any of sections 23, 24 or 24A of the Act of 1973 two copies of a draft of the order in the terms sought, one of which shall be indorsed with a statement signed by the respondent to the application signifying his agreement, and a statement of information (which may be made in more than one document) which shall include—

(a)   the duration of the marriage, the age of each party and of any minor or dependent child of the family;

(b)   an estimate in summary form of the approximate amount of value or the capital resources and net income of each party and of any minor child of the family;

(c)   what arrangements are intended for the accommodation of each of the parties and any minor child of the family;

(d)   whether either party has remarried or has any present intention to marry or to cohabit with another person;

(dd) where the order imposes any requirement on the trustees or managers of a pension scheme by virtue of section 25B or 25C of the Act of 1973, a statement confirming that those trustees or managers have been served with notice of the application and that no objection to such an order has been made by them within 14 days from such service;

(e)   where the terms of the order provide for a transfer of property, a statement confirming that any mortgagee of that property has been served with notice of the application and that no objection to such a transfer has been made by the mortgagee within 14 days from such service; and

(f)   any other especially significant matters.

(2) Where an application is made for a consent order varying an order for periodical payments paragraph (1) shall be sufficiently complied with if the statement of information required to be lodged with the application includes only the information in respect of net income mentioned in paragraph (1)(b) (and, where appropriate, a statement under paragraph (1)(dd)), and an application for a consent order for interim periodical payments pending the determination of an application for ancillary relief may be made in like manner.

(3) Where all or any of the parties attend the hearing of an application for financial relief the court may dispense with the lodging of a statement of information in accordance with paragraph (1) and give directions for the information which would otherwise be required to be given in such a statement to be given in such a manner as it sees fit.

2.62 Investigation by district judge of application for ancillary relief
. . .

(2) An application for an avoidance of disposition order shall, if practicable, be heard at the same time as any related application for financial relief.

. . .

(4) At the hearing of an application for ancillary relief the district judge shall, subject

to rules 2.64, 2.65 and 10.10 investigate the allegations made in support of and in answer to the application, and may take evidence orally and may at any stage of the proceedings, whether before or during the hearing, order the attendance of any person for the purpose of being examined or cross-examined and order the discovery and production of any document or require further affidavits.

...

...

(7) Any party may apply to the court for an order that any person do attend an appointment (a 'production appointment') before the court and produce any documents to be specified or described in the order, the production of which appears to the court to be necessary for disposing fairly of the application for ancillary relief or for saving costs.

(8) No person shall be compelled by an order under paragraph (7) to produce any document at a production appointment which he could not be compelled to produce at the hearing of the application for ancillary relief.

(9) The court shall permit any person attending a production appointment pursuant to an order under paragraph (7) above to be represented at the appointment.

Note: in courts covered by the pilot scheme, r 2.62(1), (3), (5) and (6) does not apply: see r 2.71(3)(a).

2.63 Request for further information etc
...

Note: in courts covered by the pilot scheme, r 2.63 does not apply: see r 2.71(3)(a).

2.64 Order on application for ancillary relief
(1) Subject to rule 2.65 the district judge shall, after completing his investigation under rule 2.62, make such order as he thinks just.

(2) Pending the final determination of the application, the district judge may make an interim order upon such terms as he thinks just.

(3) RSC Order 31, rule 1 (power to order sale of land) shall apply to applications for ancillary relief as it applies to causes and matters in the Chancery Division.

2.65 Reference of application to judge
The district judge may at any time refer an application for ancillary relief, or any question arising thereon, to a judge for his decision.

2.66 Arrangements for hearing of application etc by judge
(1) Where an application for ancillary relief or any question arising thereon has been referred or adjourned to a judge, the proper officer shall fix a date, time and place

for the hearing of the application or the consideration of the question and give notice thereof to all parties.

(2) The hearing or consideration shall, unless the court otherwise directs, take place in chambers.

(3) Where the application is proceeding in a divorce county court which is not a court of trial or is pending in the High Court and proceeding in a district registry which is not in a divorce town, the hearing or consideration shall take place at such court of trial or divorce town as in the opinion of the district judge is the nearest or most convenient.

For the purposes of this paragraph the Royal Courts of Justice shall be treated as a divorce town.

(4) In respect of any application referred to him under this rule, a judge shall have the same powers as a district judge has under rule 2.74(3).

Note: in courts covered by the pilot scheme, r 2.66(4) applies in an amended form: see r 2.71(3)(c).

2.67 Request for periodical payments order at same rate as order for maintenance pending suit

(1) Where at or after the date of a decree nisi of divorce or nullity of marriage an order for maintenance pending suit is in force, the party in whose favour the order was made may, if he has made an application for an order for periodical payments for himself in his petition or answer, as the case may be, request the district judge in writing to make such an order (in this rule referred to as a 'corresponding order') providing for payments at the same rate as those provided for by the order for maintenance pending suit.

(2) Where such a request is made, the proper officer shall serve on the other spouse a notice in Form M15 requiring him, if he objects to the making of a corresponding order, to give notice to that effect to the court and to the applicant within 14 days after service of the notice on Form M15.

(3) If the other spouse does not give notice of objection within the time aforesaid, the district judge may make a corresponding order without further notice to that spouse and without requiring the attendance of the applicant or his solicitor, and shall in that case serve a copy of the order on the applicant as well as on the other spouse.

2.68 Application for order under section 37(2)(a) of Act of 1973

(1) An application under section 37(2)(a) of the Act of 1973 for an order restraining any person from attempting to defeat a claim for financial provision or otherwise for protecting the claim may be made to the district judge.

(2) Rules 2.65 and 2.66 shall apply, with the necessary modifications, to the application as if it were an application for ancillary relief.

2.69 Written offers 'without prejudice save as to costs'
CCR Order 11, rule 10 (written offers 'without prejudice save as to costs') shall apply
to proceedings for ancillary relief in a county court as if for the words from 'A party
who' to 'but the offer' in paragraph (2) there were substituted the words 'Where an
offer is made under paragraph (1), the fact that such an offer has been made'.

2.70 Pensions

...

(2) Where by virtue of rule 2.62(4) the district judge has power to order discovery of
any document, he shall also have power to require either party to request a valuation
under regulation 4 from the trustees or managers of any pension scheme under
which that party has or is likely to have any benefits.

(3) No order including provision made by virtue of section 25B or 25C of the Act of
1973 shall be made unless such provision has been sought by way of—

    (a)   a form A in accordance with rule 2.53;
    (b)   a form A in accordance with rule 2.58; or
    (c)   a draft order lodged in accordance with rule 2.61.

(4) Where an application is made for an order which by virtue of section 25B or 25C
of the Act of 1973 imposes any requirement on the trustees or managers of a pension
scheme, a copy of Form A as the case may be, shall be served on those trustees or
managers together with the following—

    (a)   an address to which any notice which the trustees or managers are required
        to serve under the Divorce etc (Pensions) Regulations 1996 is to be sent;
    (b)   an address to which any payment which the trustees or managers are
        required to make to the applicant is to be sent; and
    (c)   where the address in sub-paragraph (b) is that of a bank, a building society or
        the Department of National Savings, sufficient details to enable payment to
        be made into the account of the applicant.

(5) Trustees or managers of a pension scheme on whom a copy of such a notice is
served may, within 14 days after service, require the applicant to provide them with a
copy of the affidavit supporting his application.

(6) Trustees or managers of a pension scheme who receive a copy of an affidavit as
required pursuant to paragraph (5) may within 14 days after receipt file an affidavit
in answer.

(7) Trustees or managers of a pension scheme who file an affidavit pursuant to
paragraph (6) may file therewith a notice to the court requiring an appointment to
be fixed; and where such a notice is filed—

    (a)   the proper officer shall fix an appointment for the hearing or further
        hearing of the application and give not less than 14 days' notice of that
        appointment to the petitioner, the respondent and the trustees or managers
        of the pension scheme; and
    (b)   the trustees or managers of the pension scheme shall be entitled to be
        represented at any such hearing.

(8) Where the petitioner and the respondent have agreed on the terms of an order which by virtue of section 25B or 25C of the Act of 1973 imposes any requirement on the trustees or managers of a pension scheme, then unless service has already been effected under paragraph (4), they shall serve on the trustees or managers notice of the application together with the particulars set out in sub-paragraphs (a), (b) and (c) of paragraph (4), and no such order shall be made unless either—

(a)   the trustees or managers have not made any objection within 14 days after the service on them of such notice; or

(b)   the court has considered the objection made by the trustees or managers

and for the purpose of considering any such objection the court may make such direction as it sees fit for the trustees or managers to attend before it or to furnish written details of their objection.

(9) Upon the making, amendment or revocation of an order which by virtue of section 25B or 25C of the Act of 1973 imposes any requirement on the trustees or managers of a pension scheme, the party in whose favour the order is or was made shall serve a copy of that order, or as the case may be of the order amending or revoking that order, upon the trustees or managers.

(10) In this rule—

(a)   every reference to a regulation by number alone means the regulation so numbered in the Divorce etc (Pensions) Regulations 1996;

(b)   all words and phrases defined in section 25D(3) and (4) of the Act of 1973 have the meanings assigned by those subsections.

Note: in courts covered by the pilot scheme, r 2.70(1) does not apply: see r 2.71(3)(a); references to Forms M11 and M13 are to be construed as references to Form A in Appendix 1A to the rules (not reproduced): see r 2.71(3)(f).

2.71 Ancillary relief procedure for specified courts: pilot scheme

(1) The procedure under Rules 2.72 to 2.77 shall apply to any ancillary relief application and to any application under section 10(2) of the Act of 1973 where notice of the application or notice of intention to proceed with the application for ancillary relief made in the petition or answer is filed in proceedings which are pending

(i)   in the principal registry,

(ii)   in one of the divorce county courts listed in paragraph (2), or

(iii)   in the High Court in a district registry which is mentioned in paragraph (2).

(2) The courts referred to in paragraph (1) are—

Barnsley	Northampton
Bath	Salford
Blackwood	Southampton
Bolton	Southport
Boston	Stafford
Bow	Staines

Bristol	Stoke-on-Trent
Bury	Taunton
Crewe	Teesside
Guildford	Trowbridge
Harrogate	Tunbridge Wells
Hertford	Willesden
Kingston	Wrexham
Maidstone	

(3) In proceedings to which the procedure under Rules 2.72 to 2.77 applies, these Rules shall apply with the following modifications:

   (a)   Rules 2.45(2), (3), 2.58(2), (3), 2.59(1), 2.62(1), 2.62(3), (5), (6), 2.63 and 2.70(1) shall not apply;

   (b)   Rule 2.55 shall apply with the omission of the words after 'proceeding';

   (c)   Rule 2.58(1) shall apply subject to Rules 2.72 to 2.77;

   (d)   Rule 2.60(1) shall apply

      (i)   with the omission of the words from 'A person' to 'opposite party and', and

      (ii)   with the substitution, for the words 'within seven days of service of the affidavit on him', of the words 'within eight days of service of the notice on him';

   (e)   in Rules 2.60(1) and 2.66(4), for 'Rule 2.62(5)' there shall be substituted 'Rule 2.74(3)'; and

   (f)   references to

      (i)   Form M11 or M13,

      (ii)   M12, or

      (iii)   M14

      (either alone or in conjunction with a rule) shall be construed as references to Form A, B or F respectively in Appendix 1A to these Rules and those forms shall be used with such variation as the circumstances of the particular case may require instead of Form M11, M12, M13 or M14.

References in these Rules to a rule which is modified by this rule shall be read as a reference to the rule as so modified.

(4) The procedure under Rules 2.72 to 2.77 shall apply to

   (a)   proceedings to which the President's Practice Direction of 25th July 1996 applied which were commenced before Rules 2.72 to 2.77 came into force and steps taken under that Direction shall be treated as if they had been taken under Rules 2.72 to 2.77;

   (b)   proceedings which are transferred to the principal registry or to one of the courts listed in paragraph (2) subject to any directions given by the court to which the proceedings are transferred.

(5) Where proceedings to which the procedure under Rules 2.72 to 2.77 applied are transferred to a court which is not listed in paragraph (2), steps taken under those rules shall, so far as practicable and subject to any directions given by the court to which the proceedings are transferred, be treated as if those rules had not come into force.

2.72 Ancillary relief procedure

(1) (a) A notice of intention to proceed with an application for ancillary relief made in the petition or answer; or

   (b) an application for ancillary relief;

shall be made by notice in Form A in Appendix 1A.

(2) Where an order for ancillary relief is sought that includes provision to be made by virtue of section 25B or 25C of the Act of 1973 the terms of the order sought must be specified in the notice in Form A in Appendix 1A.

(3) An application to which Rule 2.45 applies shall be made by notice in Form B in Appendix 1A.

(4) Upon the filing of a notice in Form A or Form B—

   (a) the court shall allocate a first appointment not less than 10 weeks and not later than 14 weeks after the date of the filing of the notice and give notice of that date;

   (b) the person making the application ('the applicant') shall serve a copy on the respondent to the application ('the respondent') within 4 days of the date of the filing of the notice.

(5) The date fixed under paragraph (4) for the first appointment, or for any subsequent appointment, shall not be vacated except with the leave of the court and, where such a date is vacated, the court shall forthwith fix a fresh date.

2.73 Notice in Form E

(1) Not less than 35 days before the date of the first appointment the applicant and respondent shall simultaneously exchange with the other party and each file with the court a statement in Form E in Appendix 1A which

   (a) is signed by him;

   (b) is sworn to be true, and

   (c) contains the information set out in paragraph (2).

(2) The information referred to in paragraph (1) is—

   (a) the party's full name, age, date of birth and occupation;

   (b) the party's state of health;

   (c) the dates of marriage and separation of the parties;

   (d) the full names and dates of birth of any children of the family, and the name and address of the person with whom they live;

   (e) details of the party's present residence and the occupants thereof;

   (f) a concise statement of the party's means including

   (i) his income and earning capacity,

   (ii) the value of all his assets and liabilities,

   (iii) the benefits under any pension scheme that he has or is likely to have with the most recent valuation (if any) furnished by the trustees or managers of the pension scheme pursuant to regulation 5 of, and Schedule 2 to, the Occupational Pension Schemes (Disclosure of Information) Regulations 1996, or paragraph 2(b) of Schedule 2 to the Personal Pension Schemes (Disclosure of Information) Regulations

1987, or regulation 4 of the Divorce etc. (Pensions) Regulations 1996; and

(iv) any other resources (including any resources that he may receive in the foreseeable future such as by way of inheritance), and, where an insurance policy is included, its current surrender value and date of maturity;

(g) a concise statement of any loss of widow's or widower's pension that would be suffered by either party following a divorce;

(h) a concise statement of the present and future reasonable needs of himself and any children of the family;

(i) details of the present and proposed educational arrangements for any children of the family;

(j) details of any child support maintenance assessment made by the Child Support Agency, or of any agreement for child maintenance made between the parties;

(k) a brief description of the standard of living enjoyed by the parties during the marriage;

(l) whether either party has made a relevant contribution (within the meaning of section 25(2)(f) of the Act of 1973) and, if so, a concise statement of that contribution;

(m) whether the other party's conduct (financial or otherwise) during the marriage is considered to be relevant, and if so, a concise statement of the issues of conduct relied on;

(n) any other circumstances which he considers could significantly affect the extent of financial provision to be made for the applicant or any child of the family.

The statement shall annex only such documents as are necessary to explain or clarify any of the above information.

(3) After the filing of the application for ancillary relief but before the first appointment, no discovery of documents shall be sought or given except

(a) insofar as documents have been annexed to the statement filed under paragraph (1); or

(b) in accordance with paragraph (4) below.

(4) Not later than 7 days before the hearing of the first appointment, each party shall file and serve on the other party—

(a) a questionnaire setting out any further information sought from the other party;

(b) a schedule setting out any documents sought from the other party;

(c) a concise statement of the issues between the parties;

(d) where an order for ancillary relief is sought that includes provision to be made by virtue of section 25B or 25C of the Act of 1973, confirmation that the trustees or managers of the pension scheme in question have been served and provided with the specified information in accordance with Rule 2.70(4),

and the party who served the notice in Form A in Appendix 1A shall confirm that all relevant persons have been served in accordance with rule 2.59(3) and (4).

2.74 The First Appointment

(1) The first appointment shall be conducted with the objective of defining the issues and saving costs and the district judge

(a) shall determine
  (i) the extent to which any questionnaire filed under Rule 2.73 shall be answered, and
  (ii) what documents requested under Rule 2.73 shall be produced,
  and give directions for the production of such further documents as may be necessary;

(b) shall give directions as to
  (i) the valuation of assets (including, where practicable, the joint instruction of independent experts) and
  (ii) obtaining and exchanging experts' evidence (including the holding of meetings of experts);
  (iii) any evidence sought to be adduced by each party and as to any chronologies or schedules to be filed by each party;

(c) shall (unless he decides that a referral is not appropriate in the circumstances) direct that the case be referred to a Financial Dispute Resolution ('FDR') appointment;

(d) shall, where he decides that a referral to a FDR appointment is not appropriate, direct that
  (i) a further directions appointment be fixed; or
  (ii) an appointment be fixed for the making of an interim order;
  (iii) the case be fixed for final hearing and, where such a direction is given, the district judge shall determine the level of judge before whom the case should be heard; or
  (iv) the case be adjourned for out-of-court mediation or private negotiation or in exceptional circumstances generally;

(e) shall consider whether, having regard to all the circumstances (including the extent to which each party has adhered to the rules), to make an order as to the costs of the hearing;

(f) may
  (i) in a case of urgency, make an interim order;
  (ii) with the consent of both parties, treat the appointment (or part of it) as a FDR appointment to which Rule 2.75 applies;
  (iii) in a case where an order for ancillary relief is sought that includes provision to be made by virtue of section 25B or 25C of the Act of 1973, require any party to request a valuation under regulation 4 of the Divorce etc. (Pensions) Regulations 1996 from the trustees or managers of any pension scheme under which the party has, or is likely to have, any benefits.

(2) After the first appointment, no party shall be entitled to seek further discovery of documents except in accordance with directions given under paragraph (1)(a) above or with the leave of the court.

(3) At any stage—

(a) a party may apply for further directions or a FDR appointment;
(b) the court may give further directions or direct that the parties attend a FDR appointment.

(4) Both parties shall personally attend the appointment unless the court otherwise orders.

2.75 The FDR Appointment

(1) The FDR appointment shall be treated as a meeting held for the purposes of conciliation and the following provisions shall apply—

    (a)   the district judge (or judge) hearing the appointment shall have no further involvement with the application, other than to conduct any further FDR appointment;

    (b)   not later than 7 days before the appointment the applicant shall file details of all such offers and proposals and responses to them and, at the conclusion of the appointment, any documents containing the same or referring thereto shall be returned to the applicant or respondent (as the case may be) and not retained on the court file;

    (c)   parties attending the appointment shall use their best endeavours to reach agreement on relevant matters in issue between them;

    (d)   the appointment may be adjourned from time to time, and at the conclusion thereof the court may make such consent order as may be appropriate, but otherwise shall give directions for the future course of the proceedings, including, where appropriate, fixing a final hearing date.

(2) Both parties shall personally attend the appointment unless the court otherwise orders.

2.76 Costs

At every court hearing each party shall produce to the court a written estimate of the solicitor and own client costs incurred up to the date of that hearing.

2.77 Orders

(1) Not less than 14 days before the date fixed for the final hearing of an application for ancillary relief, the applicant shall (unless the court directs otherwise) file and serve on the other party to the application an open statement which sets out concisely the nature and amount of the orders which he proposes to invite the court to make.

(2) Not more than 7 days after service of a statement under paragraph (1) above, the respondent shall file and serve on the applicant an open statement which sets out concisely the nature and amount of the orders which he proposes to invite the court to make.

Appendix 3

PRACTICE DIRECTION: ANCILLARY RELIEF PROCEDURE: PILOT SCHEME (16 June 1997)

(1) This Direction applies to all ancillary relief applications under rr 2.70 to 2.77 of the Family Proceedings Rules 1991.

(2) The Family Proceedings (Amendment No 2) Rules 1997 (SI 1997/1056), which came into force on 21 April 1997, incorporate into the Family Proceedings Rules 1991 the new ancillary relief procedure which was initially introduced by *Practice Direction: Ancillary Relief Procedure: Pilot Scheme* (25 July 1996) [1996] 2 FLR 368. The new procedure is intended to reduce delay, facilitate settlements, limit costs incurred by parties and provide the court with more effective control over the conduct of the proceedings than exists at present.

(3) A key element in the procedure is the Financial Dispute Resolution (FDR) appointment. Rule 2.75(1) provides that the FDR appointment is to be treated as a meeting held for the purposes of conciliation. Conciliation has been developed as a means of reducing the tension which inevitably arises in matrimonial and family disputes. In order for it to be effective, parties must be able to approach conciliation openly and without reserve. Non-disclosure of the content of conciliation meetings is accordingly vital. The FDR appointment is part of the conciliation process and should be so regarded by the courts and the parties. As a consequence of *Re D (Minors) (Conciliation: Disclosure of Information)* [1993] Fam 231, sub nom *Re D (Minors) (Conciliation: Privilege)* [1993] 1 FLR 932, CA, evidence of anything said or of any admission made in the course of an FDR appointment will not be admissible in evidence, except at the trial of a person for an offence committed at the appointment or in the very exceptional circumstances indicated in *Re D*.

(4) Courts will therefore expect:

- parties to make offers and proposals
- recipients of offers and proposals to give them proper consideration
- that parties, whether separately or together, will not seek to exclude from consideration at the appointment any such offer or proposal.

(5) In order to make the most effective use of the first appointment and the FDR appointment, the legal representatives attending those meetings will be expected to have full knowledge of the case.

(6) The Direction of 25 July 1996 is withdrawn.

(7) Issued with the concurrence of the Lord Chancellor.

16 June 1997

SIR STEPHEN BROWN
President

LORD IRVINE OF LAIRG
Lord Chancellor

Note: this *Practice Direction* is designed to enable parties to discuss matters openly at the financial dispute resolution (FDR) without fear that things said in mediation might then be repeated at a subsequent court hearing. The question is considered in the context of *Re D (Minors) (Conciliation: Disclosure of Information)* [1993] Fam 231, sub nom *Re D (Minors) (Conciliation: Privilege)* [1993] 1 FLR 932, CA. In that case it was held that evidence of statements made in conciliation meetings concerning children could not be given in subsequent proceedings save with leave of the court; and only then, where such statement makes it clear that the maker has in the past, or is likely in the future, to cause harm to the child.

The *Practice Direction* goes much wider than *Re D* and relates the narrow issue dealt with there, and derived from children proceedings, to ancillary relief proceedings and the FDR appointment. Public policy requires that parties be able to negotiate and put forward proposals on a basis which secures privilege for their negotiation (see **7.2** above); but the *Practice Direction* seeks to make privileged admissions made in the course of negotiations (see **7.5** above).

This leaves at large the following question: if an admission relates to something which should have been disclosed in any event, can that admission be privileged (see the requirement for full relevant disclosure enunciated by *Jenkins v Livesey (formerly Jenkins)* [1985] AC 424, sub nom *Livesey (formerly Jenkins) v Jenkins* [1985] FLR 813, HL; and see discussion in *Phipson on Evidence* 14th edn (Sweet & Maxwell, 1990)).

In *Re D* Sir Thomas Bingham MR (at [1993] 1 FLR 932, 938D–G) sets out his conclusions very tentatively and stresses the limitations of what he is saying. The judgment does not deal with admissions of fact (eg 'my mother is holding £10,000 for me' or 'I have been offered £150,000 for my family company shares'). The *Practice Direction* appears – perhaps unwittingly – to extend privilege to such admissions of fact (para (3)) and thereby in part to undermine the principle of full relevant disclosure.

INDEX

References are to paragraph numbers; *italic* references are to page numbers